D0093993

*"O Great Spirit, my one hope
Is to be worthy enough to be near You
At the end of my life on this earth!"*

Charlie Quintasket

FINDING A WAY HOME

*Indian and Catholic
Spiritual Paths
of the Plateau Tribes*

By Patrick J. Twohy

Library of Congress Catalog Card Number: 83-90797

ISBN 0-9623418-0-0

First Printing, 1983
Second Printing, 1984
Third Printing, 1987
Fourth Printing, 1990

Publisher: Patrick J. Twohy

Design/Production: Leo Aspenleiter and University Press

Typeface: Korinna
Lithography: Heidelberg Sheet-Fed Presses
Text Stock: 70# Warm White Howard Felt
Binding: Perfect-Bound on Sulby Auto-Minabinda

UNIVERSITY PRESS

E. 28 SHARP AVE., SPOKANE, WASHINGTON 99202

For Clara Covington,
For the Elders and the Young
Of the Plateau Tribes,
For my Mother and Father
And all my Family,
For my Jesuit Brothers

Table of Contents

Chapter Four
CONFIRMATION

Chapter Five
THE MASS, THE EUCHARIST

SACRAMENTS OF HEALING

SACRAMENTS OF VISION

Chapter Eight
MARRIAGE AND FAMILY LIFE

Chapter Nine
WAYS OF HELPING THE PEOPLE HOME

PRAYING

Chapter Ten
PRAYING: A WAY OF BEING IN THE WORLD

Introduction

Preface

This book was written with the help and encouragement of many friends. It is a work of respect and love, dedicated to the bands that form the Colville Confederation and all the bands of the Plateau Tribes.

It is written after ten years of listening to the hearts of both the Indian Elders and the young. It is an effort to speak for the truth. Whatever is written about Indian Ways and the Story of the People was told or shown to me by the Elders. Whatever is written about the meaning and history of Catholic Ways was explained to me by the Elders, by teachers, and by fellow Jesuits. The final writing was submitted to Elders and teachers for their approval before printing.

The transition from an oral culture to a written culture, from words spoken from the heart to words written down, is full of difficulties and pain. Each individual's unique way of seeing, remembering, and telling is lost in trying to make one poem, one story that holds together many poems and stories. One undertakes such a writing with great fear of offending any Elder's vision of the way things were and are and will be. However, I took this risk because I felt the need was so great NOW for young adults to have the chance to see a coherent and compelling Vision of the unique Indian and Catholic Spirit and Spirituality alive among their own People.

I would like to add this little work to the efforts of so many Elders to pass on something solid about their Faith in the face of an "outside" culture which threatens to sweep over the young and wash them away. The values of the "dominant" culture often have little or nothing to do with traditional Indian and Catholic values. The values of a materialistic culture leave young adults with nothing real or lasting to hang on to, and threaten to destroy them as a People.

11

If one young adult finds here something to help him sort out life's meaning and direction, I feel well rewarded.

If one young person reads something here that makes her feel very good about herself, my joy is complete.

And if this book stimulates Indian poets and philosophers to write with courage and pride about the meaning of their Indian and Catholic past, present, and future, I will then truly feel this writing has served its purpose.

Acknowledgments

I am greatly indebted to the Elders and to the young of The Colville Confederated Tribes. I thank the Elders for sharing with me the stories of their People, and for patiently trying to teach me how to live the good Way. I thank the young for believing in me and opening their hearts to me. Knowing that I can't mention all the Elders who helped me, I still want to name some:

From Nespelem: Isabel Arcasa, Mary Gua, Emily Peone, Adeline Fredin, Chuck and Agatha Bart, Shirley Palmer, Marie and John Grant, James Monaghan, Mary Pierre, Andy Joseph.

From Keller: Netti and John Francis, Joe and Marion Covington, Edward and Lillian Monaghan, Kathleen and James Burke, Archie and Rose Arnold. I wish to remember here Agnes Monaghan, who was a great inspiration to me.

From Inchelium: Louie and Cecelia Pichette, Eliza and Marcelle Bourgeau, Cecelia Smith, Geraldine Clark, Tootie and Bud Mason, Margaret and Bud Ensminger, Mary and Earl Lemery, Ada and Pete Holford, Martin Louie, Albert Louie. I wish to remember here Madelaine Desautel and Alfred Perkins who were good teachers and a joy to be with.

From Omak Area: Sue Matt, Lillian Best, Charlie Quintasket, Mose George, Alec Paul.

From Pia Mission: Mary Marchand.

I wish to thank Clara Covington (Spokane), now passed on, Frank Halfmoon (Cayuse-Nez Perce), Clarence Woodcock (Flathead), Francis Vandenberg (Flathead), for their help and encouragement in editing this manuscript. Special thanks also to Mike Paul (Colville) and Dr. Jay Miller for their helpful comments, and to Johnny Arlee (Flathead) for his friendship, example, and support.

To my fellow Jesuits living and working with the Plateau Tribes: Frs. Joseph Brown, Richard Mercy, Thomas Connolly, Jake Morton, Michael Fitzpatrick, Joseph Obersinner, Joseph Retzel, Edward Robinson, Fred Koehler, Patrick Conroy, I owe a lasting debt of thanks for their unflagging help and encouragement.

Fr. Joseph Conwell, S.J., Fr. John Steiner, Sr. Cecilia Wilms, and Maureen Foley-Bensen helped me to improve and clarify the theology implicit in the text. Fr. David Leigh, S.J., and Robert Mack helped me with the writing style. Joan Staples-Baum (Chippewa) helped me type and better organize the final manuscripts. Ms. Angela Morbeck and Sr. Glenrose Dalrymple did the difficult job of proofreading. My mother and father, Pauline and George Twohy, told me to finish what I had started: much of the writing began on their dining room table. Without the help of all these generous people I never would have had the courage or stamina to continue writing these past six years.

To the artist Charlene Teeters Raymond (Spokane), I could never adequately express my respect for the beauty of her soul and her work. I also stand in awe of Tim Schell's cover design and the sensitive, balanced art of Sam and Virginia Leadercharge (Sicangu Sioux and Colville).

I thank former Bishop Bernard Topel, Ph.D., D.D., and Bishop Lawrence Welsh, D.D., of Spokane, Washington; Bishop Thomas J. Connolly, D.D., of Baker, Oregon; Bishop Elden Curtis, D.D., of Helena, Montana; Bishop Sylvester W. Treinen, D.D., of Boise, Idaho; and Bishop Thomas Murphy, S.T.D., D.D., of Great Falls, Montana, for their encouragement and financial support. Fr. Leon Kapfer, S.J., and the Oregon Province Jesuit Mission staff were always there when I most needed help to continue. To all those who helped us publish this book I say "thank you" for your generous hearts.

All scripture quotations are from the Jerusalem Bible in English. All quotations from Rites of the Sacraments are from texts written by the International Committee on English in the Liturgy, Inc., and approved by the National Conference of Catholic Bishops.

Ways of Using This Book

This book can be used in many ways: for the joy of seeing, reading; for the adventure of dreaming, praying; for the peace of remembering, reflecting.

This book can be used to help us understand the story of our Faith, a Way of Living both Indian and Catholic. We search our hearts, asking what this Way of believing and living means to us. We ask what this Way was and is, how it came down to us, how it is lived today in Reservation communities.

In a Group

If we use this book together in a group for learning and discussion, it is good first to quiet down and pray or sing to the Holy Spirit for the gifts of understanding and peace of heart. We then read a part of the chapter we have chosen, pondering those words which in some way touched us. After this we talk about what came to us, the joy and pain of insight or memory, each one having a chance to speak. Sometimes it is good to talk about one of the questions or ideas, or one of the pictures or scripture quotations, all saying what they understand or feel. Always we finish with prayer together.

With the Young

If we read parts of this book with the young, it is good to comment on the story in our own words, telling the children our own Faith Story.

chapter one

BEGINNING TO LIVE
A LIFE OF FAITH

1. The Story of the People Searching To Find a Way Home

"By the power of an indestructible Life within them."

cf. Heb. 7:17

The Gods of the White Man

The God of the white man
Is not necessarily Jesus.
The gods of the white man
Can really be many:

Success, power, wealth,
Prestige or notoriety,
Control through mind
Of others and things,
Personal pleasure,
Looking young and beautiful,
Avoiding pain, old age, and death,
Flight from the poor, the crippled, the retarded,
Focus on clothes, booze, food, sex, drugs.

All these things
Adored by much of the dominant culture
Have nothing to do with Jesus
And are directly opposed
To traditional Indian values.

"Is Jesus white?
When we believe in Him
He becomes one of us.
Can He be dark color?

Can we judge our society?
Who judged Christ?
The Good Spirit provides wealth
And more if one is deserving.
Sinfulness is not new;

18

The Supernatural Spirit was always here
For the Indians.
New teachings blurred traditions." Clara Covington

The People Knew the Holy One

The Indian Peoples of this area
Knew the Holy Mystery
From the beginning
As the Maker, the Chief, the One-Up-Above.

"Chosen ones heard the voice
Of the Great Spirit." Clara Covington

They reverenced the old people,
The child, the Truth,
The mother-earth, the animals,
The gifts of power and beauty in each other.
They valued what Jesus valued:
Family, friendship, sharing,
Hospitality, harmony on the good earth
With everyone and everything.

Most of the Indian People from here
Were gentle, kind, and full of love,
Especially the Grandparents
Who lived with hearts wise from age.

They loved meals shared,
Laughter and long times together,
Talking far into the night
Until dawn.

They respected the time it takes
For a child, a man, a woman
To grow wise, knowing the difference
Between the really good
And the only seemingly good.

Their main faults or sins were probably
Envy, jealousy, selfishness and suspicion of each other
When things weren't going well.
This resulted in some people getting hit
And hurt or killed through the powers
Of a medicine man or woman asked or paid
By a member of a family to revenge a wrong
And to balance things out.

"There were tribal fears,
Territory battles,
Anger, envy, hate.

The Elders, the leaders, lectured,
Gave counsel, and regulated clans;
For understanding,
For peace,
And to be honorable to the Ancient One,
The Great Spirit." Clara Covington

The Coming of the Catholic Way

In time the Catholic Iroquois
Came down the tumbling rivers
Looking to trade
And finally to settle.

Before the Blackrobes were sought out
And guided by warriors
Across the great mountains to the east,
The People already knew Christian hymns and prayers,
Some in Latin.
The People had already heard from their prophets
Of the coming of a new Way.

"Among the Flatheads 'Shining Shirt'
Was such a prophet." Clarence Woodcock

"The good book,
The prayers, songs

Came with the Blackrobes
And the Bible teachers,
The Ministers." Clara Covington

The newcomers, strange men with beards
And black robes, talked the language
And traveled with the bands.
They told about a Jesus
Who died on a tree for us.
They spoke of the Creator
Who made all things.

They taught about water
That blesses with Spirit
And brings a person into heaven.
They taught the signing
With the Father, Son, and Spirit.

"The Blessed water,
Or Holy Water,
Was greatly respected.
The need for it
And the use of it
Was not like the use
Of the earliest Indians." Clara Covington

They taught about Mary,
Jesus' mother, our mother.
They spoke of saints and angels
And the place of light, the happy place
Where all would some day be together.

The People sang hymns at the Long Prayer
And took the Sacred Host on their tongues,
Food and strength for a journey to heaven.

"The People also believed
That the powers of this faith
Would complement their beliefs
And help them to be strong and brave,
Help them in their life." Clarence Woodcock

"Indian people believed
Long prayers were important.
This is not so anymore.
Now it is daily prayer,
Good works, and spiritual readings." Clara Covington

There was the Holy Book,
Filled with ancient stories,
Brought to this island
From across the big waters.
There were pictures that showed God and heaven.

The People learned about a man and woman happy,
Then miserable, wretched, thrown out
Of the good place where they stayed.
There were many stories
Of large men and monsters
And a flood that killed everybody
Except one man and his family.

"One of the first teachings
Was on Adam and Eve,
And that the God
Might punish us, too.

Obedience to God's law
Is the positive way." Clara Covington

The Indian People learned that the One-Above was angry
With His children who did not heed His word.
They learned that there was a terrible, burning place
Where bad people were sent.

"From the stories of our elders
The God the Missionaries preached about
Was one to be feared;
One that dealt punishment
And one that you confessed sins to.
The Missionaries' Mission was to drive the devil
Out of the heathen Indians,

To civilize them, make them a race of people
They did not want to be
Or know how to be." Clarence Woodcock

"The Great Spirit does not anger.
We displease Him some times,
Abusing His commandments." Clara Covington

The People were afraid.
There were earthquakes that scared
The People, and soldiers shooting
At women like they were dogs.
There were awful sicknesses
Indian medicines could not cure.

"Trembling of the earth
Is a warning by the Great Spirit:
People reform yourselves!
This is an Early belief." Clara Covington

In the midst of all this mystery and fear
There was Jesus,
Present to encourage a disheartened People.
They knew He had a Heart
Full of special love for them.

The Catholic Way Takes Root

The Chiefs and Elders of most of the bands
Accepted the Catholic religion
The Blackrobes brought. In many aspects
It was a Way much like their own.

"The religious were the peace-makers:
Their sermons on murder,
On the relinquishing of defense
And battling the invasion of settlers:
Their advice to retreat,
To receive Baptism,

To learn the church teachings,
To be saved in body and soul,
Were important." Clara Covington

They believed in this Way and lived it
Sincerely and devoutly.
The men helped build the churches
And kept discipline;
Men and women led the prayers.
The Chiefs and Elders
Encouraged their people to gather
Around the mission churches
Especially for Christmas, Easter, and Corpus Christi.

Many families ran big ranches then,
Hay and grain and fruit.
They had many cattle.
There were thousands of horses
And grass stirrup-high in the valleys.
Boys and girls were sent away for a time
To stay with the priests and sisters
At the mission schools.

"The non-Indian territory-agents
Kept head count on Indian children
In a paternalistic way.
Many Indian children
Died with broken spirits
For being detached from home and parents." Clara Covington

The First Push

The Indian people were being pushed out,
Their land taken.
They were being forced to leave the places
Where their Ancestors lived and rested.

They were being forced to go to places
They didn't know, crowded together

24

With other bands and families.
No longer was there plenty of land for everyone.

Miners combed the land
And dirtied the streams.
In the little towns Indian people
Sat by the side of the road
Covered with dust.

*"There was a mixture of good and bad
That came with the new people.
Some of the Indians described it
As the end of their world."* Clara Covington

Some of the women were treated
Without dignity.
Some of the men lay on the streets
Passed out and empty.

The Spirit, the powers
The People had been given,
Their quiet dignity
That they had known for thousands of years,
This wonderful presence
Poured out like rotten liquor
On the streets.

*"Friendship medicine,
The destructive remedy."* Clara Covington

Children were lost
Their parents lost.
The grandparents withdrew into silence
Their hearts broken.

*"Families were jostled, shuffled
Into territories called Indian Reservations
Families were divided."* Clara Covington

More settlers arrived
And the miners found gold;
The push for land continued.

The Second Push

The Indian People, who once
Moved freely over the earth
With the cycle of seasons,
Hunting, fishing, gathering roots,
Were shoved again into a smaller place.

The government gave each family
A chunk of land. They said the Indians
Didn't use their land anyway.
This was hard for the Elders to understand:
Didn't the People enjoy the land very much?
They thought the land was for everybody.
Why did someone have to own pieces of it?

The People survived.
They traveled around looking for work
In the fields and orchards.
The men worked in the woods,
Surveyed, and worked construction jobs.
They took the high-risk work
And often lost their hearing
On the heavy machinery.

*"Indians learned to be silent and withdrawn.
Indian events were told and retold
To the children."* Clara Covington

The People continued to gather
Around the mission churches.
There the priests talked and scolded
In Indian and the borrowed tongue.
The People grew to love
The Mass in Latin.

The priests told the People
Not to drink or gamble.
They told them to give up
Their Indian medicine powers.

"The non-Indian introduced the fire water.
For some of the Indians
That was a questionable, forbidden thing,
Something evil, evil." Clara Covington

The priests saw the bad in Indian medicine,
Men and women jealous, quarreling,
Killing each other with fear.

They did not see the good side of the medicine,
The powers given for healing and strength.
Many of the People buried their medicine bundles
In the earth, never to go back to them,
But others did not bury their bundles.

"The powerful spirit lingered,
Kept secret in private ceremonies.
Some disposed of their symbols or bundles." Clara Covington

The People Continue On

There were some good times.
There were enough old people
Who knew something,
The right way of doing things.

People seemed to get along.
Work was hard: long, long hours
Dawn till evening.
There was little money
And just enough to eat.

"Indians, like children,
Learned what money was." Clara Covington

The People still looked Indian.
They felt toward the earth
And towards each other in that way.
They wondered, should they act white
To avoid being ignored, insulted, laughed at?

27

"The new surroundings, the schools,
Slowly changed the Indian Way." Clara Covington

The People continued on,
Many now with white and Indian blood.
Many grandparents went only the Catholic way.
Some kept to the old ways.
Some believed in Church
And still kept the Winter Medicine Dances
And the older medicine ways,
Hoping the priest would not find out about it.

"Some Indians left the Catholic
And joined other Faiths." Clara Covington

The Chiefs had made an agreement
With the Blackrobes,
Land for schools, a church,
A new place for the People
To camp together,
To be happy and pray together.
The Chiefs were searching
For a sense of direction
In the midst of a sea of confusion and pain.

"Later on they also agreed with the Sisters
To have a hospital in St. Ignatius
Always for the Indian." Clarence Woodcock

"There is a great challenge in Christ's way:
'So that all might be one'." Clara Covington

The Blackrobes had a dream
And the power to carry it out.
They had begun in earnest
Together with the Sisters
To work with the boys and girls.

They wished to share with the children
The gifts of speaking, reading, writing,

28

Counting, in the way the outsiders did
Who surrounded them.

The priests felt
That if the Indian People could not
Speak, read, write,
They would always be oppressed.
They wished the People to be able
To hold their own in the midst
Of a dominating society
That threatened to engulf them.

But this learning came
At a great price.
Children were separated from their grandparents.
This made a gnawing, hurting emptiness,
A loneliness inside.
A whole Way of life was ending.

In the school the children were demanded
To speak in the borrowed language.
They began to forget their own tongue.

"My Aunt recalls the time
She was captured by the Blackrobes
And brought to school.
Her father rescued her.
She speaks of that time as if enemies
Were capturing their children.
She said it was not good." Clarence Woodcock

The grandparents grew silent.
They talked to each other
But no longer to the children
In the old way.
This was very sad.

"Endurance and survival,
With joys, sorrows,
A passage through domination and damnation.

Some were saved in peace,
Others lost, drowned in tragedies." Clara Covington

Most grandparents felt the priests
And sisters were really trying to help.
Even though some priests and sisters were cruel at times,
Many were wonderful, warm, and kind.

Even the grandparents wore shoes and hats
And clothes of wool and cotton.
They knew a way of life was passing,
But they wanted their children to survive.

The Coming of the Wars

Eventually the *Second World War* came.
This time almost all the men went away.
Some died over there
Across the waters—
Our brothers, we never saw them again.
The women worked in the shipyards.

Some men came home,
Wounded and heroes.
They never talked much
About what happened.
They drank a lot. It got
So nobody gave a damn.

There was just drinking,
Wrecking cars, marriages broken,
Children abandoned,
Funerals every week.
You could not have a gathering
Without drinking going on.

The old people seemed unable
To stop it.
They became silent.

They were losing all their children.
They would go to church to pray
And no one would be there with them.

There was no good news.
The grandparents' eyes were
Always full of tears.
But they kept on living.
Maybe only one of their children
Would finish school, go to church,
Stay home with their family.

"All of thls appears later.
The Second World War was not too damaging;
Indian families prayed together.
The Holy Spirit was everywhere
In these times. Military men returned
With less or no evil." Clara Covington

And Then There was Korea

The young men went again;
They were full of courage,
Taking the missions
No one else would take.
They were still hunters and warriors,
Not afraid of death.
Some came back in sacks or pieces,
Some never came back.

"Here was the beginning of madness
With the Indian people.
The Holy Spirit was fading
From many of the Indian People." Clara Covington

Congress wanted to relocate the People
Off the Reservation
In places like L.A.
Where they could work on asembly lines.

31

Congress hoped to terminate the Reservations.
Big money was talked about.
The people turned on each other.

It was the same old game;
Divide and conquer.
But enough people wanted
To hold onto the land.

If there was no land,
There would be no treaty rights,
No place where you were from,
And no place to go home to.

"The war and evil grew,
Meaning unrest and despair for many;
Faith, Hope, Love diminished.
Families in separation
Knew hardship and loneliness.
Indian people with inner doubts
Began to withdraw from the church
And the teachings.
This was Indian land
And now we were drowning
In our captivity and foreign affairs." Clara Covington

There was Viet Nam

The young men asked
For the heaviest fighting,
For the place of danger.
Many were wounded and lost.

This time it was worse.
Besides the bullets and blood, there was
Heroin, cocaine, grass,
And booze. The war seemed
Without end or meaning.

32

"Parents and children separated.
Parents continued to pray and believe;
The children began to lose Faith." Clara Covington

The men came home from a nightmare
That wouldn't leave them.
Some in their own country
Rejected the sacrifice they had made.

The men bore the tragic burden
Of knowing that many of the Vietnamese
Killed, were as innocent and hunted
As their own Ancestors were
A century before.

"The 'do or die' military training
Twisted our sons,
Our children of the Second World War.
They came home drugged,
Wined, changed men,
Useless, pitiful.
These witnessed the war zone.
Many others returned normal." Clara Covington

At home in the schools
The children continued to receive
The century-old message:
The Indian People
Were merely an obstacle to progress,
And westward expansion.

It became obvious to the kids,
After countless western movies,
That it was better to be a live cowboy
Than a dead Indian.

The Indian People Today

Where are the Indian People today?
In the last ten years the Others

Have proclaimed that it is all right,
Even fashionable to be an Indian.

"The madness of being controlled
Pressed the World War generation
To protest in their life style.
This generation went back to braids, beads,
Back to Indian Rituals with Indian chants." Clara Covington

They say Indians are not necessarily
Dirty any more,
That Indians should not only vote
But also run their own affairs.

The non-Indians feel that Indians can drink
In their dark bars
And even swim in their motel pools.

The Church feels saddened and confused
By what has happened.
She wishes now to encourage the People
To follow good and lasting Indian ways
That are the gift of the Spirit to them.
Well, maybe it's too late.
In some places the language is almost gone.

"Many Indians changed churches
And withdrew from the Catholic.
The early teaching said the One Catholic Church
Is true, holy, and apostolic,
That it does not err.
Then the Mass changed
And religious garb.
The religious dine, wine, and dance.
What happened to God?" Clara Covington

Being Indian Is?

What does it mean to be Indian today?
Does it mean long, black hair,
Grey eyes, Navajo jewelry,
And cowboy boots under a three piece suit?

Does it mean feathers at Mass?

Does it mean hopping around at war dances
In Plains Indian gear?

"Indians caught on to fashion and fads.
The Earliest Indian did not expose
His ceremonial feather gear.
This was serious gear,
For battle and victory." Clara Covington

Can there really be a stick game
When both the pointers are drunk?

How do you keep a Sweathouse
In a new housing project?

How do you visit with friends
Over a loud TV?

How many politicians would make speeches
About the value of being Indian,
If it didn't mean pleasure and power
And money in their pockets?

"The Indian learned to be competitive
In the classrooms.
With 'no trespassing' on what were hunting,
Fishing, and root-gathering areas,
The only thing left to do
Was to compete for an Indian program job.

If Indian lands become taxed,
Indian self-esteem may drown too." Clara Covington

35

Does being Indian mean
That no one ever grows up?
That no one can give up the endless
Round of tournaments and parties
To spend a little time with their kids?

"The Indian learned fashionable entertainment
From his peers.
The Indianness of just being home with children
Has gone out. In some cases
Grandparents are sunk in the cycle
Of modern society." Clara Covington

How much can the grandparents stand
Before they completely disappear,
And there is nothing?

nothing

NOTHING!

Except the same opportunity they had
To give thanks,
To participate,
To sacrifice,
To endure hardship.

The same opportunity to see
The good and the Holy
In children and the old folks,
In food and in all creatures.

The same chance
To feel joy and sadness,
To sing and dance,
To be whole and strong,
To speak from the heart.

The same chance
To be open and friendly,
To forgive and love,
To not drink or drug
The Spirit away.

The same opportunity
To be hospitable and kind,
To feed and shelter the stranger, the poor,
To be faithful in love.

Is there not the same opportunity
To care for parents,
To listen to grandparents and elders,
To see they are not forgotten?

Is there not the same chance
To always have plenty to give away,
To welcome those who have no family,
To look down on no one,
To respect the right of each one
To feel, to speak, to choose?

Is there not the same chance
To guide and correct the children,
To show them a good Way,
To be something for them to see,
To hold onto, when their world
Turns upside down?

And is there not the same opportunity
To pray in the morning and evening,
To give thanks before meals,
To speak, when old enough,
Something good for the People to hear?

And is there not the same chance
To tell a daughter, a grandson,
That the Jesus
The great-great-grandparents knew,
Is the perfect Response of their Creator
To their great joy
And endless sorrow?

"The old way stood for teaching
Spiritual things to the children

At a very early, nursery age.
Then Knowledge of good and evil
Becomes part of life for them,
And Knowledge of the Holy Spirit,
Or Great Spirit, always a part of them,
To help them in major decisions." Clara Covington

The same opportunity
To tell the children
That Jesus is the Hope of the living
And the dead,
The People Then, Now, Forever
United inseparably in His Heart.

To tell the children
That when they look at Jesus on the cross
They look at their own Indian People.

"Which was more cruel,
Christ's crucifixion or slaughtering masses
Of Indian people for their lands?
This is almost too great to compare.
The Indian people are the most downtrodden
Among human creatures, we dare say.
We cannot glory in any Indian Saints." Clara Covington

Their People, bloody, covered with wounds,
Yet lifted up by the Creator
For all the world to see;
His Indestructible Life within them
Streaming out like sunlight,
Expanding without limit,
Lasting
Forever.

2. The Joy of Finding Him

*"The Kingdom of Heaven is like treasure hidden
in a field which someone has found."*

Mt. 13:44

One of the most important things in us
Is our capacity for happiness.
Each one of us,
From the severely wounded or retarded
To the most gifted and brilliant,
Has a special capacity for happiness.

The secret is to find out
What makes us most deeply happy.
Perhaps, for some of us it will mean
Hard work, self-sacrifice, pain, all
Challenging our endurance, our capacity to grow.
Whatever it is, when we have found it
We have found a great treasure.

Our Lord asks us to give away everything,
To walk a path of selflessness.

We can be happy in many ways;
Comfort, pleasure, excitement,
Having a lot of time and things for ourselves.

But the question is,
When are we most deeply happy?
Are we happy having a lot, hoarding,
Or giving away, having little?

The point is
When we have given everything away,
We might find Him
Whom money, status, power,
The best connections in the world,
Cannot buy.

He is a free gift,
A treasure hidden,
That neither time nor death
Can take away from us.

He is always there
Waiting to be discovered in our hearts,
When all the layers
Of everything else
Less real and good,
Have been given away.

He is always there,
Waiting to be discovered in the rich hearts
Of those who really have nothing.

3. The Price of Following Him

"Happy you who weep now: you shall laugh."

Luke 6:21

We are often afraid of pain,
Yet when we are in pain
At least we know we are alive.

We are often afraid of death,
Yet out of death
Good can come, and Life.

We are often afraid of solitude
Because of the emptiness we feel,
Yet He is always there to fill us with power.

We are often afraid of being tested
Beyond our strength to endure,
Yet He is always there to walk with us.

We are often afraid of trusting,
Of giving our lives over to Him,

Yet all we are and have
Finds its Ground to grow in Him.

We are often afraid to give up our plans
Though they are always near-sighted and incomplete,
Yet time and again He shows a willingness
To guide and protect us.

We are often afraid of others,
Yet only they can mirror back our goodness
And love us into Life.

We are often afraid to give away everything,
All that we are and have,
Yet that giving would fill us
With wealth overflowing.

We are often afraid of the pain of loving,
Afraid of reaching out,
Yet without this pain we die.

We are often afraid to stop worrying
About ourselves, about what we have
And how important we are,
Yet unless Our Lord can free us
From the slavery of self-preoccupation,
We never will really See
The beauty that continually surrounds us.

We are often terrified we won't have enough
To eat, to wear, enough magazines,
Movies, parties to keep us happy,
Enough noise to keep away the quiet.
Yet unless we are helped to let go of these things,
We will never discover the sweet taste of Silence
Or the joy of meeting ourselves for the first time.

We are often afraid to be with the violent,
The confused, the ugly, the forgotten,
The simple, the down-and-out,

Yet they are a mirror of ourselves, the image of
Our situation before God in this world.

We often want to throw up a wall
And sit well-fed and drunk in our private garden,
Where we can't hear the immense cry of pain
That surrounds us from all our starving
And slaughtered brothers and sisters.
We often want to knock ourselves out
With booze or drugs or sex or comfort,
We are so afraid of the truth the pain in and around us
Might teach us about ourselves.

We find ourselves in a battle.
We want to get off the front lines
And go to a little beach somewhere
And lie in the sun-warm sand
And forget it all.

Yet there is really no place
Out of this world.
And the one persistent question
We are always asked inside
Will never go away, for it is a question
We will be asked forever:

"Did you take care of My brothers and sisters?"

4. Death Is Our Constant Companion

Death is our constant companion,
A companion that most of us
Would rather not have.
It is he who makes life
Both intolerable and precious.

Death is intolerable to those of us
Who begin to fear the inevitable,

The deep pain of sorrow
With the loss of our family,
Our friends, our People.

But death teaches us
To take nothing for granted,
Not today, not tomorrow,
Not health, not good fortune,
Not home, family, and friends.
Everything and everyone is subject to death.

Death teaches us that each moment
Is precious and will never be given again,
That we are here on borrowed time.

The old person who shares wisdom with us,
The young person who reaches out in friendship,
The man who lies broken in the street,
The child who looks to us
With eyes hungry for love,
All may leave us tonight.

We have to say "goodbye"
So often in our lives.
Each time it hurts deeply
And the empty place in our heart
Never really fills or heals.

If we did not hope to say "hello"
Again in our Creator, our desire to love
Would seem totally betrayed.

5. The Light Within Us

"You are the light of the world."

Mt. 5:13

Let us dare to say
That in the midst of awful stillness,

43

In the midst of anguish, darkness, emptiness,
There dwells complete, mysterious Light.

This is the Light
That forms our minds and hearts.
This is the Light
That falls on the words
Of our mouth
Making them alive and shining.

This Light is ready to emerge, break forth,
Even through the most broken
Minds, hearts, and bodies.

Light wishing to be born,
To be as it is,
Wonderful, Peaceful, Alive.

This Light within us and within all things
Needs to be enkindled
By our feeble acts of love,
Our emptiness, our reaching out.

Yet It is always there,
Greater than the force of a thousand suns,
Ready to shine through our eyes,
Tired with weeping,
And lighten up the whole world.

6. Could We Dare to Say?

Could we say
That in the beginning
There was this unimaginable burst of Light,
And then came the Earth and Sky,
The Animals,
Then the People and all things?

Could we say
That in the middle of time,
When all that were waiting stood still,
Both above and beneath the earth,
We were visited by One so little
And so tall
That He inhabited the Heavens
And the Earth at once?

Could we say
That at a moment in time
This same burst of Light that began all things
Blew this man terribly beaten
From death to Life?

Could we say
There has been released
An Energy so awesome and unexplainable
That it still carries and defends,
Shakes and judges
Every man and woman that ever was
And ever will be born?

And could we say
That at the end of time
This Light, this Life, this Energy
Will so blow through the entire universe
That it will be changed into something entirely else;

That there will then be
Fullness of Light unimaginable,
Fullness of Life unextinguishable,
Fullness of Love unexplainable?

Could we dare to say all this?

chapter two

THE MEANING OF SACRAMENT

*Everything is what it appears to be
And more than what it appears to be.*

1. The Meaning of Creation

What Is Created Is Good

All creation is good, holy.
It is only what can come out of the hearts
Of us humans that makes it unholy
And a reason for despair.
For a man or woman whose heart is right
All things are good
And reveal the good Heart of the Creator.

The Battle Between the Spirits

For us the spirit world is real.
Good spirits, or angels,
Are our Creator's continual delight.
They are our allies, our helpers
In our struggle to keep our hearts
Open, warm, and generous.
They work always to keep all creation holy.

Evil spirits, the fallen angels
Who turned away from the Face of our Creator,
Belong to Satan, their leader.
They are always at war against us
Trying to make our hearts small, cold, and selfish.
They try to tear us to pieces
And convince us our lives are worth nothing.
It is the work of Satan and the evil spirits
To turn the universe into a nightmare of terror
In which we destroy each other
And the whole earth.

The Creator Lives Among Us

In the midst of this struggle

The Creator of all has come to our rescue
With the gift of His own Heart to us,
The man Jesus.
Because Jesus' Heart is so completely full of love
For us and for all things,
He has given us and all creation a Holy Spirit
Whose power can lift us far beyond the limits
Of our human weakness and defend us
From the attacks of Satan, the Enemy.

This Spirit given by Jesus to the universe
Breathes into it a Life that will change it
Into an entirely new Reality,
Once the kernel of the creation we now know
Has split and fallen away.

The Gift of Faith

We come to see all this
Through the eyes of Faith.
Faith is the Creator's gift to us
Of Light to See
More than just what meets our eyes.

Faith happens when our Creator suddenly
Pries open our hearts
By some act of kindness towards us
Through the world within and around us.

The Sight given is of a world
Where generosity and mutual love,
Honesty and respect,
Kindness and forgiveness are all possible.

This Faith is a Vision of ourselves and our world
Forever struggling with forces within and around
To give birth to an entirely new Self
And an entirely new World.

2. The Meaning of Creation for the Ancestors and the Great-Grandparents

The Ancestors

For the Ancestors,
The holy, ancient ones,
The whole universe held within and above it
The very Presence of its Maker.
This was a Presence clothed with Mystery,
Ready to break forth at any moment
With manifestations of terrifying, awesome power
And healing Love.

This was the Maker
Whose gifts of guardian spirits
And healing foods and water
Sustained the life of the People
For thousands of years.

The Great-Grandparents

For the great-grandparents
Who heard and held the Word, Jesus,
In their hearts,
This Maker also became the Presence of the man, Jesus,
Whose Heart, now freed
Through His suffering and death for His People,
Was as wide and long and high and timeless
As the universe itself.

The great-grandparents not only knew
The Holy Mystery in and above
All they saw, heard, touched, tasted,
But also the Presence of Jesus
Whose Heart held them and all created things
In a future full of hope, in a place called
Heaven with all those who had gone before them.

We Today

It is this Holy One, the Maker,
Whom we call Father.
It is this Jesus,
Whom we meet in the Heart of all people and things,
Whom we call Savior.
And it is Their Holy Spirit,
Whose Love draws us together and sustains us,
Whom we call our Guide and Protector.
It is They, together with all of the holy ones
In heaven and on earth,
And all that is good and holy in and above the earth,
That we invite to be in and with us
When, in a most intense and deliberate way
We gather to pray in the sacred manner
We have come to call Sacrament,
The prayer of the Creator's People, the Church.

3. Grace and Sacrament

Looking back after the Resurrection
The Disciples realized more deeply than ever before
That the Heart John felt beating
When he put his head on Jesus' breast
At the Last Supper,
Was the Heart of the Creator of All,
Given, Present, in the Center of, all creation.

Grace

Grace is the Fullness of Life freely given
And received by a heart full of thanks.
It is the Fullness of Love freely given
And received with tears of thanks.

Grace is all creation
As the Creator's gift to us.
It is through creation

That the Creator holds, touches,
And talks to us all the time.

When we stand before the sun,
Listening to the clear sounds of morning,
Or dive into the cold stream,
Or eat good food, or touch another person
With genuine care for them,
We behold, we hear,
We feel, we taste and touch
The Creator who is active in all things,
Filling them with life.

Sacrament

A Sacrament is a holy moment
In which we come into harmony with the Creator
And all creation.
A Sacrament is a sacred moment
In which grace is given and received.
It is a moment in the journey of our life
In which we experience our hearts opened
By the love of creation for us.
It is a moment, sometimes of great pain,
In which we are helped to know ourselves
As if for the first time.
It is a moment in which we begin to See or Feel
The Life-giving Presence of the Creator, our true Home,
The Love-giving Presence of Jesus, our real Freedom,
The Light-giving Presence of the Spirit,
Our lasting Strength and Peace.
It is a moment in which our friendship
With angels and saints
And the goal of our journey, Life with them,
Becomes real for us.

Sacraments of the Church

The Sacraments of the Church are special moments

In which Jesus, working through His Holy Body on earth
Gathered as a Family to pray,
Unites us to Himself in a most intense way.
He unites us to His death and Life,
Death to sin and Life in the Spirit.

To do this, Jesus uses some of the simplest
And most beautiful things He has given us:
Water, oil, bread,
Our hearts, voices, and hands.

We Catholics name Seven Sacraments:
Three Sacraments of Entry into the Church,
Baptism, Confirmation, Eucharist;
Two Sacraments of Healing,
Reconciliation and The Anointing of the Sick;
And two Sacraments of Vision,
Marriage and Family Life,
And Ways of Helping the People Home.

Sacramentals

Sacramentals are holy things:
Heat from sacred fire or stones,
Smoke from incense, cedar, or sweetgrass,
Light and candles, water that is blessed,
Feathers, fir and cedar boughs,
Statues, medals, bundles,
Rosaries, clothes, bells.
They are anything good that helps us to pray
And to feel our Creator's Presence in and around us.

*   *   *   *   *   *

There is much more that could be said
About the meaning of Creation
And the meaning of Sacrament.
But perhaps now we can best adventure
More deeply into these mysteries
By searching into the meaning
Of the Sacrament of Baptism.

chapter three
BAPTISM

*"I Baptize You in the Name of the Father,
and of the Son, and of the Holy Spirit. Amen."*
From the Rite of Baptism

(In Trying to Understand Baptism
It is Helpful First to Consider
What It Means for an Adult to Be Baptized.)

1. Indian Ways That Are Related in Meaning to an Adult's Coming Into the Church Through Baptism

What Were Some Things
Water Meant to the People?

All bands shared the water
Of the big rivers
And the streams that ran into them.
Each band camped together
By the waters of certain rivers and lakes.

These waters meant Life for the People:
Water for salmon to come home in,
Water for drinking and cooking,
Water for the joy of bathing, swimming,
Water providing protection and distance from enemies,
Water for travel in dugout canoes to relatives and friends,
Water in which to feel close to the Creator of all,
Water in which to see one's self as one truly was.

How Did a Stranger Become One of the People?

From times way back
To become one with a band or tribe,
To enter into the sacred ways of a People
Was a most solemn and serious undertaking.

Persons had to know what they were doing.
They had to understand well the traditional
Way of life of the band or tribe they
Wished to participate in.

They had to show they were ready
To take their part, their role
In the life of the People.
Their words, deeds, actions
Were carefully observed by the People.

A person had to be accepted by the People
Fully as one of their own,
One who would follow their ways
Faithfully, with great respect,
Generously giving and providing
For the good life of everyone in the band.

The person learned more deeply that
One's whole life was a prayer,
Giving thanks for all the earth's gifts,
Praying in a Sweathouse for health and purity,
Entering the pure and cleansing stream

"To wash away earthly stains of misdeeds." Clara Covington

2. Indian Christian Ways for an Adult's Coming Into the Church Through Baptism

"Jesus replied: 'I tell you solemnly,
unless a man is born through water and the Spirit,
he cannot enter the kingdom of God:
what is born of the Spirit is spirit.
Do not be surprised when I say:
You must be born from above.
The wind blows wherever it pleases;
you hear its sound,
but you cannot tell where it comes from
or where it is going.
That is how it is with all who are born of the Spirit'."
John 3:5-8

What Does Baptism for an Adult Mean?

Baptism is a rebirth into a new way of life.
It is leaving an old life behind
And coming into a new one.

Will Baptism Cost Us Something?

Even if this means suffering
Physical pain, worry, weariness, death,
We accept this as part of our calling,
A participating in Christ's sufferings,
In the pain of the world
Yearning, groaning to be freed.

Why Are Those Desiring to Enter the Church Anointed With Oil? What Does It Mean?

In the anointing with oil
We wish to show that we want
Jesus' help and power
To be Christians, that we wish to follow
Christ's life, trying to imitate Him very closely,
Sharing in the pattern of His life,
Hoping to overcome our selfishness
And the powers of the Evil One
At work in the world.
The People pray that we might become free
From all that keeps us from close union
With our Lord Jesus.

We wish to give up our lives for our friends,
Striving to love even our enemies.
Willing to live, and work actively
To make a world more just and good and holy
For our children
And for all God's children.

What Time of Year Is It Best
For an Adult to Be Baptized?

We carry this hope within us
That if we live and die with Jesus,
Our kind Father will also raise us from the dead with Him.
Therefore, Lent leading towards Easter,
The time of the Church's most intense participation
In the suffering, death, and resurrection of Jesus,
Is the most fitting time
For an adult to be baptized.

What Happens to Us When We Are Baptized?

To be baptized presupposes that we
Have pondered deeply the mysteries of our Faith.
Humbly hoping to proclaim our Faith
Together with the whole Christian community,
We ask the Saints to help us.

It is in this spirit then
That we receive the waters of Baptism,
Desiring to be a new person,
One who wishes to leave the sinful person behind
And put on the new person, Christ Jesus, our Lord.

Forgiven and washed clean,
We receive God's Spirit fully in us.
There is really only One Baptism:
Jesus' suffering, death, and resurrection.
This Baptism we enter into through our Baptism
Of water and the Holy Spirit.

We participate in the Baptism of Jesus
Through our suffering, death,
And resurrection together with Him.

What Does Our Confirmation
After Baptism Mean?

After our Baptism, the priest or Bishop
Lays hands on our head
And anoints us on the forehead
With the Holy Oil.

The whole community prays for us
That we might be completely strengthened
And filled through the outpouring
Of Jesus' Holy Spirit upon us.

This anointing is the sign
Of our dignity and completeness
As God's own son or daughter.

What Hope Does Our Baptism and Confirmation
Place in Our Hearts?

In the new union we have with Christ
We hope to become
Persons of deep prayer, goodness, and leadership,
A great hope and joy for the whole community,
A light shining in our world.

What Is the First Thing We Do
After Our Baptism?

We now join the rest of the community,
Our Christian family,
At the Eucharist, sharing with them
The strength of communion with our Risen Lord.

A Wonderful Thing About Us

The most wonderful thing about us
Is that we are meant to live forever.

This is what our Baptism means:
That if we enter fully into what it is
To be human, to love, to suffer,
To give ourselves away,
We become one with our Lord
In doing this.

And when we have given away everything,
He will welcome us home in heaven
To be forever with all those
We have deeply loved
As we journeyed around this good earth.

3. Indian Ways That Relate in Meaning To Our Tradition of Baptizing Babies

How Was All Life Seen?

From the beginning
All life was seen as good and holy and joined together.
The whole mystery of human life coming into the world
Was held in great respect and reverence.

In What Ways Was Life Prepared for and Received?

Young women were prayed for and prepared carefully
To be mothers. They tried to remain strong,
Holding to a healthy diet, prayerfully remembering
Their dedication to Life, to their People.

Grandmothers with powers for healing and life
Helped bring babies into the world
With great skill, understanding, and tenderness.

Babies were a treasure
In the eyes of parents and grandparents.

They were a gift, the continuing
Life of the family and band.
Grandparents asked for the children
Long, healthy, useful lives:
Gifts which needed the help of a Vision.

"In the Indian way,
Infants were highly accepted as a gift
From the Spiritual Providence.
The earliest Indians
Presented their infant to the very old,
Aged great-grandfolks, for prayer, offering,
And as an act of Hope
That the Great Spirit might
Come upon this child;
Meaning, may this child
Seek a Vision in purity,
And may this child be received
By the Great Spirit for Medicine Powers.

It is the Grandparents
Who prepared a child for the seeking
Of the Great Spirit
For the Indian Medicine Powers." Clara Covington

How Was the Child Kept Healthy?

The child was carefully nourished and kept
Healthy with food and medicines from the earth.
Warm and secure on his baby board,
He was surrounded with beauty and love
Because he was beautiful.

"In the earliest days of the Indian People
The grandparents anointed infants
In humility and perseverance
As an act of hope.
For example, one of the family was requested
To hunt and slay a pheasant.
With a part of the pheasant

The infant is anointed on the head
For patience and understanding.

For the body, there might be a hunt
For a small animal like a chipmunk.
The animal oil is rubbed or anointed
On the sole of the infant's feet
That he might be alert and cautious
In his chosen paths.

These ways were relinquished
With the arrival of the new people,
And the introduction of the Church
And all its teachings." Clara Covington

"There are many medicines:
Heart of grouse makes a person
Warm-hearted, kind, but slow;
Bees make them hard workers, etc." Clarence Woodcock

What Was the Meaning of the Gift of a Child?

The child brought the family together
And continued its life.

The child was the promise of someone
Who would care for parents
When they were old
And remember them
When they were dead.

The birth of a child was a great joy.
In the hearts of parents and grandparents
There was a spirit of giving thanks
To the Maker.

63

How Was the Child Taught?

"The Indian way
In the initial teaching
Was done as an act of hope
That a child would respect creatures:
Plants, the forest, the wind,
Because the Divine Spirit can and will
Speak to his earthly child
Through an earthly means." Clara Covington

4. Indian Christian Ways Concerning The Baptism of Children

"Think of how God loves you!
He calls you his own children,
and that is what you are."
1 Jn. 3:1

What Are We Doing as Parents When We Bring Our Child for Baptism?

When we bring a child to be baptized,
We say for the child what we hope
He or she will want to say as an adult;
Hence, we are taking a serious responsibility.

What Is It We Want to Say to God? What Do We Ask Him for Our Child?

We wish to thank our Creator for our child,
To dedicate the child to Him,
For the child is holy as He is Holy.
We realize with reverence how treasured a
Gift the child is to us, how sacred, how fragile.

We ask our Father-Creator to protect the child,
To keep it healthy, good, and holy. We wish

Our child to be filled with the very Life of God,
God dwelling in our son or daughter—
Father, Son, and Holy Spirit.

Why Do We Bring Our Child Into the Church For Baptism?

In bringing our child to Church for Baptism
We show our desire that this child be brought fully
Into the Christian life of our community.
We pray that he or she will join
All these young people,
Parents, and grandparents
Who believe in God and His Church
With their whole heart and soul.

What Promises Do Parents Make To Help Their Child?

The child does not yet know the community of belief,
The Christian family,
That he or she is being brought into.
The parents, therefore, in love and fairness to the child,
Resolve to help their child to know
The great Mysteries of our Way
As the child grows older.

It is in this spirit
That parents have always wanted their children
To spend time with their grandparents,
Hoping their child will learn and grow,
Surrounded with the love, wisdom, and holiness
That only grandparents can share.

Parents ask the Creator humbly
That they will be leading a life together
In which their child will be able to see
The Creator's goodness and love.

If the child senses that his parents
Do not believe in our Creator
And love the Creator in each other,
He will have a hard time learning
To believe that our Creator is good,
A merciful and kind Father of us all.

"It is parents who lay the foundations
Of honesty, respect, fairness, and love,
So that when the child develops his reasoning powers,
They will be positive." Frank Halfmoon

How Do Parents Choose Godparents For Their Child? Why Does the Child Need Godparents?

Godparents, then, are chosen with great care.
It is the godparents, together with grandparents,
Who will help the parents
To teach their child Jesus' Way.
They, together with the parents, are meant to be
The mirror of God's love for the child.

If parents should die, or fail in their duties,
Godparents continue caring
For their godchild's well-being
And help the child to know and follow Jesus' Way.

"Among the Flatheads,
The godparents chosen
Were those respected for being
Good, wise, and strong." Clarence Woodcock

5. Some Symbols Used in Baptism

Water

Life comes from water.
Cleansing is done with water.
It is a sign of cleansing from sin
And any tendencies towards sin.

It is a sign of new Life.
A person comes out of water
Clean and new.

Water is also a sign of the unknown,
Of the Abyss, of the depths of darkness,
Of death.

We enter into the waters of suffering and death;
We sink, we drown, we die;
And yet we rise up again.

In union with Jesus
We pass through suffering and death
Into Life Forever!
He has done this for us.
He has gone ahead of us!

White Garment

*"You have become a new creation and have clothed
Yourself in Christ. See in this white garment
The outward sign of your Christian dignity."*
Our Creator is like the pure, clear light of the sun and sky.
The new white garment placed
On the person after Baptism
Is a sign of the new person who wears it,
Full of God's Light and Peace.

Candle

"Receive the light of Christ . . .walk always as a child of Light."
Like Christ, who is the light of the whole world, the candle
Reminds us to keep the light of faith burning in our hearts
So that our lives will shine like His.

Oil

"I anoint you with the oil of salvation . . ."
Since olden times oil has been used for cleaning, healing,
Warmth, and light. In the Old Testament times, oil was
Used to consecrate things and persons like Kings,
Prophets, and Priests. Anointing with oil
Brought the person into contact with the
Sacred Presence of the Creator. Anointing was related to
The gift of the Holy Spirit. The word *Christ* means
"Anointed One." Quotations from the Rite of Baptism

6. How Did We Come to Have Baptism?

What Was the Meaning of Baptism In the Early Church?

The early Church chose Baptism
As the effective sign
Of a new Believer's entrance into a life
Of union with our Lord
And with His Body, the Faithful Community.

The Baptism was the sign
Of the believer's entrance into the Mystery
Of Christ's death and resurrection.
This made the believer
One with Christ's Body, the Church,

And, therefore, filled with the Life
Of that Church, the Holy Spirit.

Through Baptism the new believers
Became brothers and sisters of Christ,
Heirs of all the Gifts of His Spirit
In this life, and in the Life to come,
Co-heirs with Christ of God Himself.

Why Did Baptism Spread Throughout the World?

After His death and resurrection,
Jesus appeared to His disciples
On a high mountain in Galilee.

He told them:
"Go, therefore, make disciples of all the nations:
Baptize them in the name of the Father
And of the Son and of the Holy Spirit;
And teach them to observe
All the commands I gave you.
And know that I am with you always;
Yes, to the end of time." Mt. 28:19-20.

And so Jesus sent out His disciples
To Baptize all those who would come to believe
In the Name of the Father, the Son, and the Holy Spirit.
After the disciples had received
Jesus' Holy Spirit,
They went out to the whole world
To share what they had
Heard and felt and seen.
They baptized all those who came to believe
With water and the Holy Spirit.

How Did Baptism Come Down to Us?

And so Baptism spread
Throughout the whole world,

69

To all tribes and nations,
Coming down in history towards us
Through all the generations of men
And women who believed in Jesus
And His saving power right into our present.

We, today, with faith in Jesus,
Filled with His Holy Spirit,
Pass on the greatest gift
Our parents and grandparents shared
With us, our Faith,
Baptizing our children
And our brothers and sisters in the name
Of the Father, the Son, and the Holy Spirit.

In What Spirit Do We Carry on This Tradition?

We carry on this tradition
With great gratitude and humility,
Knowing that our Baptism
Is our Creator's free gift to us
Out of His love and mercy for us—
A share in His own Life, forever.

*" . . . It was for no reason except His own compassion
That he saved us, by means of the cleansing water
Of rebirth and by renewing us with the Holy Spirit
Which he has so generously poured over us
Through Jesus Christ our Savior.
He did this so that we should be justified
By his grace, to become heirs
Looking forward to inheriting eternal life.
This is doctrine you can rely on."* Titus 3:5-8.

7. A Note on the Rite of Christian Initiation of Adults

In the Rite of Christian Initiation of Adults
The Church today has restored for us
The Catechumenate of the early Church.
The Rite brings out the full dignity, beauty,
And meaning of an adult's coming into the Church.

This Rite is a source of strength and blessing
Both to the persons coming into the Church,
And to all of the Faithful; for by helping
Their new members to Faith,
The Faith of all is strengthened.

The Precatechumenate

The full Rite of Initiation includes
Four periods of growth. The first time of growth
Is called the precatechumenate.
During this time the persons seeking Faith
Become acquainted with the Christian community
In which they live, learning about our Lord through
Prayer and Scripture, meeting Him in the lives
Of the Faithful. If they are given the gift of turning
To our Lord and desire to follow Him more closely,
They are invited more fully into the believing community.

In a ceremony before the faithful, the men and women
Desiring entrance into the Church tell of their wish
To follow our Lord and renounce all other worship.
They are prayed for by the community, signed with the
Sign of the Cross, given their Christian name,
And welcomed to begin a more intense time
Of preparation: The Catechumenate.

The Catechumenate

The Catechumenate is a time for finding our Lord
In prayer, learning about Him
Through the study of Scripture,
And studying in depth the Church's teachings
And traditions,
Especially her view of herself and her role in the world.

Catechumens, the ones receiving instruction,
Should learn especially about our Lord's law of loving
Even our enemies,
About sin, repentance and forgiveness,
All of the sacraments,
And about the liturgical life of the Church
Throughout the year.
They should be helped to join gradually into the worship
Life of all the Faithful.

This time of preparation can take a year to three years
To complete. During this time Catechumens
Are prayed for often, and blessed
So that they can continually be more
Free of anything that holds them back from
Our Lord. When the Catechumens feel prepared to ask
For a further step, they are again called before the Faithful
During the Eucharist. Their names are
Enrolled and they are chosen to proceed into the most
Intense period of preparation: the time of Purification.

The Time of Purification

This time of Purification usually takes place during Lent.
During this time the Catechumens
Are brought forward before the People several times
And are prayed for that they might
Be freed from all that keeps them from close union with
Our Lord, Jesus Christ:

Christ the Water of Life,
Christ the Light of the World,
Christ the Resurrection and the Life.

During this time, they are entrusted with two prayers
Dear to the Church: The Our Father, which teaches us
How to pray, and the Apostles' Creed, which tells us of the
Faith of the Church.

The Sacraments of Initiation

At the end of this time of Purification, the Catechumens,
Usually during the Easter Vigil, are formally received
Into the Church, the Body of Christ,
Through the Sacraments
Of Baptism, Confirmation, and the Holy Eucharist.
In Baptism they are joined to Christ's Life.
In Confirmation they fully receive the Spirit He promised.
In the Eucharist they share Him, together with all the
Faithful, through the Bread broken and given.

After Baptism

After this Event, the new members of the Church,
Usually during the Easter Season, are honored and
Encouraged to ponder the Holy Mysteries they have
Entered into, and to enter ever more deeply into
Their community's life of Faith and helping others.

8. A Note on the History of Baptism In the Church

Why Do We Have Baptism? How Did It Get Started?

In the first century after Jesus' death and resurrection, Baptism was an outward sign of a person's turning from sin and giving himself to Christ. It included a time of instruction and preparation. The person was received into the Christian community through a bath of water and sometimes the laying on of hands.

How Did the Ceremony of Baptism Change and Grow? Was Confirmation Part of Baptism?

During the second through the fifth centuries, candidates for Baptism were asked to undergo a long time of preparation, a time for prayer, learning, fasting, and good deeds. The candidate had a sponsor and was prayed over and anointed so that evil powers would be driven out of him. He entered into water naked to be baptized and, after coming out, was given a clean, white garment. He was then confirmed or strengthened in his faith by an anointing from the Bishop. Because the Bishop was unable to attend all Baptisms, in the Western Church this final anointing was given later in a separate ceremony of Confirmation.

When Did the Baptizing of Babies Begin? How Do Church Leaders Look at Baptism Today?

From the sixth to the fourteenth century, Christianity became the common belief of the European world, and so the Baptism of infants became the normal thing. This practice has lasted right up to the present day. Since 1962 and the Second Vatican Council, Church leaders have brought the Rite of Adult Initiation or Baptism into the forefront, with its insistence on a long period of preparation so that the person can truly learn about Christ and begin living like Him. For the Baptism of babies, careful instruction of parents and godparents in the meaning of Baptism is considered most important.

9. Prayers the Church Entrusts to Adults Seeking Baptism

The Apostles' Creed

I believe in God, the Father Almighty,
Creator of heaven and earth;
And in Jesus Christ, His Only Son,
Our Lord; who was conceived by the
Holy Spirit, Born of the Virgin Mary,
Suffered under Pontius Pilate,
Was crucified, died, and was buried;
He descended to the dead; on the third day
He arose again; He ascended into Heaven,
And sits at the right hand of God,
The Father Almighty; from thence He shall
Come to judge the living and the dead.
I believe in the Holy Spirit, the
Holy Catholic Church, the Communion of Saints,
The forgiveness of sins, the resurrection
Of the body, and life everlasting.
Amen.

The Our Father

Our Father, who art in heaven,
Hallowed be Thy name;
Thy kingdom come, Thy will be done
On earth as it is in heaven.
Give us this day our daily bread;
And forgive us our trespasses as we
Forgive those who trespass against us;
And lead us not into temptation
But deliver us from evil.
Amen.

chapter four
CONFIRMATION

Be sealed with the Gift of the Holy Spirit."
Amen."
Peace be with you."
And also with you."
from the Rite of Confirmation

"I shall give you a new heart,
And put a new spirit in you;
I shall remove the heart of stone
From your bodies
And give you a heart of flesh instead.
I shall put my spirit in you
And make you keep my laws
And sincerely respect my observances.
You will live in the land
Which I gave your ancestors.
You shall be my people
And I will be your God."

Ezekiel 36:26-28

1. Indian Traditions
   That Relate in Meaning
   To the Sacrament of Confirmation

How Were Young People Prepared for Taking Their Place as Adults in the Band or Tribe?

In times long ago,
Before young men or young women
Were ready to take their part as adults
In contributing to the ongoing life of their band or tribe,
They were given a time of careful preparation
For their duties as husbands and fathers,
Hunters, leaders, warriors; or as
Wives, mothers, and weavers, working with their husbands,
Providing for their families, holding together the camp
And the whole way of life of their People.
They were expected to know
The wisdom and the ways of their People
Handed down to them through the stories and legends
Of their Grandparents. They had to show
They were ready to use whatever skills and powers
They had been given by the Animals
As Spiritual Messengers—
Powers given for building up the life
Of their families and the whole People.

How Did Young People Find Their Roles in Life?

There were times for prayer and fasting;
There were times out alone in the mountains,
Acts of hope for spiritual communication.
There were dreams, songs, and visions,
And, with their elders, times for spelling out
The meaning of these dreams and visions.

The elders tried to see and to teach

Each person's role or way of being in the world.
They helped them bring out their song,
And gave them their names.

What Way of Life Were They Taught?

Young men and women had to learn
What times, places, and things were sacred.
They had to know how to live in solitude
And how to live with others. They were taught
Respect for themselves, for all living beings,
And especially respect for their Elders.

They learned to be strong and pure.
Facing the morning sun, they gave prayers of thanks
And bathed in the cold stream.

*"They prayed in the Sweathouse
To the Great-grandfathers, the deceased,
Like to the Communion of Saints."* Clara Covington

These were times of great discipline,
Great prayer, and meaning. This was before
The Interruption and the beginning of the time
Of great sadness and confusion.

How Did a Young Man Find Himself
And Come to Know His Helping Power?

Sometimes the men would take a boy out
Into the wilderness. He would sweat with Elders,
Then fast and pray for three days alone,
After which he would seek counsel with his Elders
To better understand the significance
Of what had happened to him while he was out alone.

*"For those who had no 'Vision,' there was
An interpretation by which the Elders*

79

Could counsel the young man to a wise use
Of his trial.
Each one who did this received some spiritual aid
Which lasted his lifetime." Frank Halfmoon

During these days the purpose of a young man's life
Might come clearer to him.
If his faith was positive,
Powers might come to him, and his song
Be placed deep within him.
At another time his spirit guardian
Might declare a message to him,
Perhaps when he was sick,
Or in danger, or at the Winter Dance.

How Did a Young Woman Find Herself
And Come to Know Her Helping Power?

The young girl, too,
When she became a woman,
Would be taken apart from the people
For brief periods of training.

She, also, would be purified and cleansed,
She would fast and pray. She would be taught
The meaning of her life as wife and mother.

She would know times of solitude in the wilderness,
And learn her skills for bringing life into the world.
Her song would come to her and, perhaps,
Powers for prayer and healing
Hearts, minds, and bodies.

"If their faith was weak
Failures or an evil spirit could overtake the young;
Then Spiritual gifts
Could not be had or received." Clara Covington

80

2. Some Indian Christian Ways To Consider in Preparing for Confirmation. What Does It Mean to Live a Life Filled With the Holy Spirit?

"I shall ask the Father,
And he will give you another Helper
To be with you forever,
That Spirit of truth
Whom the world can never receive
Since it neither sees nor knows him;
But you know him
Because he is with you, he is in you." John 14:16–17

"The Wilderness the young go out into
Today, is the fearsome, complex, wild
Society that threatens to overwhelm them." A Colville Elder

Who Am I? What Can I Do to Help?

Who am I?
What can I do to bring peace
When members of my own family cannot get along,
When there is envy, jealousy, bad feelings
Between families, when some of my brothers and sisters
Are drunk all the time?

"Drunkenness is a confused retreat and solitude,
An imaginary comfort." Clara Covington

What can I do when children are abused
Or left to be lonely,
Sniffing gas, smoking dope, drinking?
What can I do, who can I be?

It will be important for me
To find time alone

81

To be by myself
Just myself before my Maker,
Alone, outdoors, riding my horse,
Walking, thinking, praying,
Hoping to become pure in my heart
So that I can be of help.

"It is important that I understand who I am;
There is a deep-seated urge
To do something good for my people.
Before that, I have to know myself,
My weaknesses and strengths,
So I can be a better instrument.
This assessment does not do anything
But list the qualities which identify me.
Once that is done, then I'm ready
To correct mistakes, to fortify the body and mind.
Then my prayers have more meaning." Frank Halfmoon

What Ways are Part of Me?

"The non-Indian society says
That I should prepare to leave my family
By the time I'm 18 or 21.
They do not understand how important it is
For us to be with our family.

It is in the family that we learn
Patience and understanding.
It is there we receive valuable advice
About teachings that have been lost
And how to continue on into another age." Clara Covington

My heritage—
The gift of my grandparents and great-grandparents—
Is wide and great and is
Without time, it goes back forever . . .

To be good and kind,
To have reverence and respect

For every living creature,
To thank our Maker, our Father,
For everything He gives me . . .
Thankful that I can be happy and sad,
Have much and have little,
Live and die,
And live again in the good place.

What Can I Hope to Be for My People?

I will try to learn what I can
To love and protect the land we live on
And all the animals that share this land with us,
To share whatever I have with
My family, my friends, my neighbors.

When someone does not live or speak honestly,
I will try to speak out for what I hope
Is best for everyone. I wish to keep the land
Good for everyone. I wish to regard each person
With respect, as much as I can.

I will try not to drink or smoke so much
That I lose my clear mind,
My respect for myself and others,
So I won't be or do what makes me miserable
Or ashamed and makes me want to die.

And I will try to be kind and patient
With those who drink, and offer them
My hand when they fall, asking for help
To get up again.

I will try to keep myself pure
And healthy and strong
So that when I am married
I will bring my whole self
Proudly and without shame
To the one partner I will want
To join me on my walk through life.

I will learn everything I can
In and out of school
So that I can someday be able
To protect and provide for my children.
Looking carefully
At other couples I know,
I will try to learn what builds
And what destroys a marriage.

I will watch carefully the children in our town
Trying to see what in their parents
Hurts them and causes them to be sad,
Withdrawn, lonely, confused, lost, angry;
And what in their parents causes them
To be content and happy, out-going,
Trusting, peaceful, at home.

"Not all marriages are blessed with children,
So any children in a family are to be cherished
As a special gift. Their upbringing
Shouldn't be left to someone else,
To foster homes.
Childhood lessons should include
Large daily portions of attention,
Understanding, love." Frank Halfmoon

How Will I Walk Before My Father?

Everything I do I will do for
Our Maker, our Father:
Dancing, singing, walking,
Loving, praying, working,
Resting, enjoying, hunting,
Fishing, camping, playing,
Eating, waking, sleeping.

What Does God's Spirit Do Within Me?

The Holy Spirit in me
Will make me want to sing,
To be whole,
To be good,
To be pure of heart,
To be full of strength and life,
To bear wrongs patiently.

The Spirit in me will make me want to dance,
To help out others,
To be thankful,
To be sorry for my sins,
To be happy and forgiven,
To be full of light and peace,
Calm and steady.

Each morning, facing the sun,
I will thank our Father for the gift of this day,
Hoping to live in harmony with Him,
With the earth, with every living being.

How Can I Protect Our Reservation Land?

This is our land.
This is where we were born.
We will live here and
We will come back here to die.
This is our land. We must care for it
And keep it beautiful.

There will have to be decisions made
About our land, about the minerals in it,
The trees upon it, the animals that share it with us,
Teaching us how to live in harmony with the land.

We will have to be smart
To think the right way,

To make the right decisions—
Not to make the land ugly,
Not to make our town ugly
To make a few people rich.

Rather, we should treat the land well
So that everyone has enough for a good
Home and family, enough to share
Around so that fathers and mothers
Can work and provide for their children.

This is our land.
It is still ours to protect and defend.
I want it to be beautiful.

"If I have Faith in the Indian God,
The Great Spirit,
Then I certainly might pray
My act of Thanksgiving
That I have an Indian Reservation.

I should pray sincerely
That my great Spirit, the Divine Providence,
Will reward me with an earthly abode
And all the changing beauties that go with it." Clara Covington

"While this land may be called Reservation,
It is ours because of special laws.
Our grandparents and their grandparents understood
The laws of Nature and lived accordingly,
They knew the penalty of waste,
The benefit of natural supply and demand." Frank Halfmoon

What Can I Do for Our Town?

"This is our town,
Where we live and do our trading.
We like to have an atmosphere of friendship.
All those who live and work here

Represent the community in their actions.
We all benefit when our community is a place
Where friends meet; where there are no lines
That mark 'privileged' places." Frank Halfmoon

"Here I am free to exercise my earthly foolishness,
Neglecting my spiritual gratitude.
Here I am free to thank God for the comforts
Of this town where people can meet
And gather together." Clara Covington

This is our town
Where we live together.
Many bands and tribes, many peoples,
We share this place together.
Working together makes it a good place to live.
When we work divided, it becomes a
Hateful, empty place.

How Can I Help One Who Is Not an Indian?

There is much that has not been good
Between the Indian and the White Man.
The white man has sometimes been cruel
And greedy and hard:
He has been without knowledge and compassion.

But some white men were good and fair and kind.
Even today there are white people
Who are sorry and ashamed of what happened.
They would like to understand Indian ways better,
But they need to be patiently taught.

They need to be forgiven and helped.
They need the friendship of the Indian more than ever.
They need to learn to see, to feel as the Indian does.
They need to learn the way of the heart
And its own language.

"For these many years the Indians
May have appeared passive
To all the surrounding noise
Made by a variety of neighbors.

Yet the People have been active
In their daily pursuits, passing on
Tribal history and lore to those in the family.

If now we are still strange
To our white neighbor, I wonder
Whether there is more the People should do.

Now is not the time
To cease practicing patience;
There are values worth striving for
In each society." Frank Halfmoon

What Was It Like at the First Meeting?

In the first day of their meeting,
Indian, Blackrobe, and White Man
Met with equal strength. They had
The eyes and heart of respect for each other.
They stood strongly in each other's presence.

Ignorance, war, and greed
Put an end to that, and the endless
Years of sadness, confusion, bitterness began.

Now the days are coming again
When Indian, Blackrobe, and White Man
Stand once more as equals.
Each needs the other to live.
There can again be mutual respect and love.

What Can I Do for People When They are Down?

It hurts us all when our brothers and sisters
Drop out of school,

Lose their jobs,
Lose their families and wander lonely,
Get thrown in jail.

It hurts us
When our brothers and sisters are humiliated,
Made fun of,
Looked down on as
Second-class citizens,
Drunken Indians.
This is not really funny.
It is no good for anybody.

I will try to keep in touch with those
Who drop out, who lose their family.
I will visit those who get thrown into jail,
So they don't lose hope.
I will drop off some candy and cigarettes
And bring them home,
Give them clothes
And help them start again.
I want them to have a chance
To start again and have somewhere to go.

"To understand one who is down
Is a special gift.
Many times a dear one loses footing
On this trail of life.
Not everyone is blessed with a way
For words. We who have thumbs
For tongues can show our love by genuine concern,
By showing that we really do care." Frank Halfmoon

Whom Do I Look Out for When I'm Having Fun?

When I play sports
I will not be satisfied
Until I have done my best
And helped each of my teammates

To look good and play together.
I will encourage my opponents to play
As well as they can and congratulate them when they win.
When I see someone in school
Or downtown, or at the community center,
Whom no one likes, who is left out, lonely,
I'll talk to him or her and try to care,
Showing the person he is still worth attention,
That she is all right being who she is.
I'll try to include them
In what my friends are doing.

Somehow I know
They will turn out to be
My most genuine and generous friends.

3. How Can I Participate in All the Sacraments of the Church?

What Do I Do When I Go to a Baptism?

When I go to a Baptism
I realize that the baby or the grown-up person
Is becoming one of us, that in
A special way he or she
Is God's own son or daughter
Full of grace, light and peace,
Full of goodness and the Holy Spirit.

I resolve, with all the people present,
To be a good example for the baby
Or my friend, and care for the one baptized
As part of my own close family,
Hoping that he or she will see God in me.

Why Do We Need the Sacrament of Confession Or Reconciliation?

We need to forgive
And be forgiven.
Often we hurt others
Just seeking what pleases us.

We treat others as objects to be drawn towards us
Or pushed out of the way
As we feel we need or don't need them
For our own "happiness."
We don't treat others as persons
To be loved, respected, cared for.
We walk through our Father's creation
Using things, using others,
Never giving thanks.

From the beginning
The People never took anything
Without giving thanks.
When a hunter killed a deer
He made a song of thanks.
When the first salmon of the year
Was netted, the people gathered together
In ceremony to give thanks
For the return of the salmon.

Why Do I Go to Mass?

We should give thanks every day
For family, for friends, for everything.
I go to Mass to give thanks.
I am glad to be in Jesus' Presence
Among His people, calling to mind
His great power to love and forgive.

I listen to his teachings.
I offer myself, my whole life,

As a prayer to our Creator, our Father,
Together with Jesus, the Great Priest,
And all the priests and people.

I ask to be filled with His Holy Spirit
And to be together with Jesus and His people
In Holy Communion, sharing His strength
To go out and work for a better world.

What Does Marriage Mean to Me?

When I am married
I will want to say to all my friends,
To the whole town, that
This is the one I love and cherish
Just the way God, my Father, loves and cares for me,
Just the way Jesus loves His people, the Church.

*"I will want the world around to know
That my life is shared by one
Who helps me, loves me, cares for me.
This one I honor in the Presence of God."* Frank Halfmoon

I will say that I will love this person
Forever, no matter what we have to go through.
Together we will work for our children
And everyone's children.

Our home will be a place where
Someone can come
Who has no other place to go.

What if I Become a Prayer Leader or a Priest?

And if I become a Prayer Leader or a Priest, a Deacon,
A Song Leader, a Reader, an Assistant to the Priest,
A Teacher, a Person of deep Prayer and Healing,
I will try to learn everything I can

About our Creator and about being human.
I will try to love all people
As if they were my own brothers and sisters,
My own family.

I will try to be like Jesus
As much as I can, seeing if I can help out,
Feeling and knowing when people hurt,
Enjoying life with them when they are happy,
Giving my whole life and energy
So that kids and all people are more free,
More happy and full of hope,
Trying to be honest about myself,
Standing up or even giving my life
For what is true and right.

I will bring Jesus, our Lord, to the People
In Mass and Communion,
At Wakes and Funerals,
Baptisms and Marriages,
Accepting loneliness and rejection,
No longer living my own life,
But letting the Power of Christ
Live in me.

"This loneliness and rejection
Is something I fought for a long time
(Even turning to alcohol)
But I couldn't handle it.
Once I accepted it,
Life was/is much better.

This could be a word of advice
To others still searching.
Then we wouldn't be lonely,
As we'd all be special,
Sharing the Love of God." Clarence Woodcock

How Can I Care for the Old and the Sick?

When people are old
And shut in,
I will visit them, cut wood for them,
And clean their houses. I will help the priest
To bring them Communion,
Wanting them to know they are special in my eyes.
I will listen to the old stories,
Learning what is greater than having money
Or things, learning the things that last forever:
Faith, hope, and love.

When someone becomes very sick
I will bring the Prayer Leaders and the Priest
So that they can join the family in prayer,
Blessing, comforting, and Anointing the sick person,
Asking the Holy Spirit
To strengthen him for his continued journey here on earth
Or his journey into heaven.

What Can I Do When There Is a Death?

If someone dies
I will want to be there
To help him or her on the journey to our Creator.

Consoling the family, I will bring food
For the dinner, sing and pray during the Wake
And, in the morning, offer Mass and Communion for the
One leaving and for his family still with us.

At the final meal together
I will pray and be glad that
Everything is being completed.

If there is a Give-Away
I can recall with everyone present
How precious is the life
Of the one who went ahead of us.

"Even if I were not a prayer leader
I would want to go sit with the family,
Knowing from experience suffered
That even my presence
Helped wipe a tear
And warmed a heart full of agony." Clarence Woodcock

Why Do We Clean Graves Every Spring?

It is good to love and respect those
Who have gone before us.
We clean their graves every year
To show our feelings for them:
That we have not forgotten them, that we are
Grateful for their struggle to live, grateful
For all they handed on to us.
We reaffirm our close bond with them
And seek again their goodwill towards us.

4. What Happens at Confirmation Time?

What Does a Person Want to Feel
And Say at Confirmation?

At Confirmation I will tell the Bishop
And all the People that I wish to be a Christian,
That I wish to follow Christ's Way,
To follow Him as closely as I can.

I will want to give my life
To do everything I can
For my family,
My friends,
And all my People.

I will look to the example of my Sponsor,
Someone I have carefully chosen,

Someone in whom I see what is Holy,
Someone whose life of Faith
I wish to share more fully.

I hope to walk toward my Great-grandparents,
Traveling the same good path
That leads to eternal life with them.
There will be slips and falls,
But I hope to keep getting back up
And going forward towards them.

All of this I do
With the hope
That if I live and die with Jesus,
I will also be raised from the dead with Him
By our kind Father.

What Happens to Us During The Confirmation Ceremony?

During the Mass for Confirmation
We are called by our Name
To go before the People, to express our common faith.
We stand before the Bishop,
The Prayer Leaders, the Priests,
Our Sponsor standing by our side,
Hand on our shoulder.

The Bishop, Prayer Leaders, and Priests
Extend their hands over us
And, together with the whole people,
Pray that we receive the Holy Spirit.

The Bishop then anoints us
With Holy Oil:
The Sign of the Holy Spirit
In us and with us,
The sign that we belong to our Creator
In Jesus forever.

We now join the rest of the community
At the Eucharist, sharing with them
The strength of Communion with our Risen Lord.

5. Some Words for Confirmation Sponsors to Hear

We Are Looking

These days we have more things.
We seem to control our lives more.
We don't seem to need our Creator.
We don't sense His Presence
In each other, in the Earth and Stars.
We don't often feel Him within us.
Older words and songs that stirred
Our grandparents' hearts
Fail to move us.

Perhaps we need a new language
For our situation, our times;
We believe, but we do not feel
The meaning, the heart, of the Old Ways.

We Need Someone

We need someone to guide us
And be our friend;
Someone to help us
Find ourselves
Our hearts
Our language
Our experience of the Creator of all.

We need someone who will stand by us
And listen to us,

97

And help us up when we are down;
Someone who will love us
And be patient with us.

We Need Something NOW

There can be no turning back for us.
We must find our lives
Sacred, Holy, now, in the present,
Weaving carefully what is old
And what is new, how we knew the Creator
In the old days, and how we know
Him now, weaving beautifully,
Strongly, the three strands
Of the one braid of our experience:
The Indian, the Christian,
The totally new and unexpected.

We Can't Be Someone Else

There can be no turning back
Into what is less than ourselves.
There can be no empty gestures
Or mouthing words
That we do not know the meaning of.

We are engaged in a struggle.
Many of our companions have died.

If we do not really find
A purpose for living,
We will die, too, and
Our people will grow weaker
And more full of sorrow.

There Is This Hope in Us

We're looking for a time
When our people will feel

Really good about themselves,
When we will all pull together
And work together
Toward the good of everyone.

We're working toward a time
When we will feel proud of ourselves,
At peace with ourselves and with one another,
Walking in dignity
And harmony with all that is true
And good and lasting.

There Is This Prayer in Me

I ask my God to give me a heart
That knows what is true about myself
And what is false, what is building
And what is destroying;
What is from the Good Spirit,
The One who seeks to bring me life,
And what is from the Evil Spirit,
The one who seeks to destroy me.

It will be helpful for me
To know someone Wise
Who can recognize and point out
The movements of these spirits in me.

6. When You Go Out Alone Into the Hills to Pray

When you are out alone in prayer
Everything that happens in and around you
Is very important.
Notice everything you think, feel,
See, hear, touch, smell.

Become aware of yourself and your surroundings
And become aware of all your experiences
Which, like clouds passing by in a clear sky,
Come and go.
Let each thought, feeling, sensation
Just happen to you, and when it is finished
Let it go on freely
Like a leaf in sunlight, floating downstream.

Relax and be yourself.
If you feel like dancing or singing
Do this. If you feel like talking to yourself
Or to the Holy Ones, present in you
And in all things, do this.
Relax and rest often
Just looking at the sky, the trees,
Feeling the wind, the sunlight,
Listening to all the sounds and silence around you.

Know this, that you are not alone.
You are surrounded with life that loves you,
Everything that is trying to praise the Creator
By being fully itself. Each tree, each flower,
Each bug or bear is a being
Aware of itself and all other things.
You are not alone.
Be at peace. Let your mind
Empty itself out, let your body relax.
Be at home here where you are.
Do not wish for a moment to be anyone else,
To be anywhere else but HERE NOW!

If you wish to think, then think hard,
Your head down as you walk.
And when you are tired of thinking,
Let it go.
If you want to worry, then worry hard for awhile,
With your forehead wrinkled, your stomach, shoulders
And chest tight, your body tired, nervous, and heavy.
Then let your worry go.

For awhile just be your ears.
Listen as if you had no eyes.
If you wish, cover your eyes for awhile.
What all do you hear?
What do you notice about the place where you are?

For awhile just be your eyes.
Be as if you could not hear.
What do you see?
What do you notice about the place where you are?

For awhile just be your sense of touch;
No eyes, no ears.
What shapes and textures do you feel around you?
What do you notice about the place where you are?

If you wish, just hold in your mind and heart
Or say slowly to yourself a single word
Like *Jesus.*
Do this for awhile.
Or say very slowly a prayer you know
Or read a little from your book
And let the words be inside you.
But you are surrounded with life,
A book always around you,
All you have to do is learn to read it.

Stand, arms out, facing the sun
And pray for strength for yourself and your People.

Pray by the stream or river
For a pure mind and body, calm and clear,
So that Power might flow through you
To help your family, your People, all Peoples.

Touch the earth gently with your feet—
She may have a message to give you,
To help you.
Behold and touch everything that grows on her
And consider the miracle of Life,
How it moves in a circle from death to life.

Notice the sky above you—
What does the sky tell you?
And your companions the trees—
What feelings do they have for you
And you for them?

Notice all that lives around you,
Sharing Life with you—
The animals big and little, the birds.
What do they wish to share with you?
What secret do they wish to tell you?
Notice everything, everything is important!
Even the little fly sees himself central to everything
Around him and finds himself important.
Everything and everyone is important!
The rocks and the mountains—
They will talk to you
If only you become calm
And very quiet.

For whatever you notice in you
That is not full of light and freedom,
Ask the earth, the sky, the trees,
Everyone and everything, for forgiveness.
Humbly ask our Creator
To send His Spirit to heal you, to fill you
And make you new and free.

What you notice in you good and shining,
KNOW THIS, ACKNOWLEDGE THIS,
Shout your prayer of thanks,
Relax and be happy in this.
Thank the Creator for living in you,
Working through you in a wonderful manner.

Life is completely a gift, precious and fragile.
Live THIS DAY in a beautiful manner,
Walking humbly, honestly, full of love and thanks
For everyone and everything.
You will never be here this day again;
These moments will never be given to you again.

Try to notice and be thankful for everything
That happens in and around you.

Know that you are here, alive in this way,
On this earth for only a short time.
You are just passing through.
All of your hungry and suffering brothers and sisters
In the world need your walk through life
To be pure, unselfish, loving, kind, honest,
Always mindful of them.
Know that what you see and touch,
What you hear and walk on,
Was loved by your Ancestors for thousands of years.
Know that they are still with you and await you.
Walk then, full of dignity and self-respect.
Walk full of honor and reverence for all things.

Love yourself and love everyone,
Even those turned away from you.
Walk as a Hunter of Life:
Your path goes from this life into the next.
Walk as a Hunter of Truth,
The truth about yourself and every living thing.
Walk as a Hunter of Light,
And be filled with Light and Peace.
Amen. So be it!

7. How Did the Sacrament of Confirmation Come Down to Us?

How Did Jesus Pass on His Holy Spirit to His Disciples?

When Jesus knew He was soon to die,
He called His disciples together
To tell them
He must soon go to His Father,

The One who sent Him.
The disciples were worried
So Jesus tried to encourage them:

"Yet you are sad at heart
Because I have told you this.
Still, I must tell you the truth.
It is for your own good that I am going
Because unless I go,
The Helper will not come to you;
But if I do go,
I will send him to you." John 16:6-7

Jesus, in trusting obedience to His Father,
Did give up His life for those He loved
To pass on His Spirit to them.
After His Father had raised Him from the dead,
He appeared to his disciples
And told them to wait
For the Spirit He had promised.

"When He had been at table with them,
He had told them not to leave Jerusalem,
But to wait there
For what the Father had promised.
'It is,' He had said,
'What you have heard me speak about:
John baptized with water
But you, not many days from now,
Will be baptized with the Holy Spirit'." Acts 1:4-5

When Did the Apostles Receive the Holy Spirit?

And as He had promised, right
After His Ascension into heaven,
Just fifty days after
Their Last Supper together,
Jesus sent His Holy Spirit
Down upon His disciples
On Pentecost (a word which means
Fifty days after the Passover):

"When Pentecost day came around,
They had all met in one room,
When suddenly they heard what sounded
Like a powerful wind from heaven,
The noise of which filled the entire house
In which they were sitting;
And something appeared to them
That seemed like tongues of fire;
These separated and came to rest
On the head of each of them.
They were all filled with the Holy Spirit,
And began to speak foreign languages
As the spirit gave them
The gift of speech." Acts 2:1-4

What Did the Gift of the Holy Spirit Do to the Apostles?

After they had received
The gift of the Holy Spirit,
The Apostles, once afraid
Even to go out onto the streets
For fear of losing their lives,
Became filled with great faith,
Power, and courage.
They preached the good news
Of Jesus' resurrection from the dead
Openly, without fear;
And went about doing the works of Jesus
With great strength,
Healing people and delivering them from evil spirits
Through the power of His Name.
The followers of Jesus
Became a living Church.

What Were Some of the Gifts the Holy Spirit Gave to the Early Church?

The tremendous variety of gifts
The Spirit gives to the Church

Is witnessed to by St. Paul
When he gives this teaching on
How we should view the gifts of the Spirit.

"There is a variety of gifts
But always the same Spirit...
The particular way in which the Spirit
Is given to each person
Is for a good purpose.
One may have the gift of preaching
With wisdom given him by the Spirit;
Another may have the gift of preaching instruction
Given him by the same Spirit; and another
The gift of faith given by the same Spirit;
Another again the gift of healing,
Through this one Spirit;
One, the power of miracles; another,
Prophecy; another the gift of recognizing spirits;
Another the gift of tongues and another
The ability to interpret them.
All these are the work of one and the same Spirit
Who distributes different gifts
To different people just as He chooses." 1Cor. 12:4-11

St. Paul was also well aware
Of what in us is opposite
To the work of the Holy Spirit:

"When self-indulgence is at work
The results are obvious:
Fornication, gross indecency
And sexual irresponsibility; idolatry and
Sorcery; feuds and wrangling,
Jealousy, bad temper and quarrels;
Disagreements, factions, envy;
Drunkenness, orgies and similar things...
What the Spirit brings
Is very different:
Love, joy, peace,
Patience, kindness, goodness,
Trustfulness, gentleness, and self-control." Gal.5:19-21,22-23

106

How Was the Tradition of Confirmation Passed on to Us?

In the early Church
When someone was ready
To become a Christian,
The Apostles, after Baptism,
Laid hands on the person and, together with the
Whole community, prayed that
He or she might receive the Holy Spirit.
And so this tradition has continued
In different forms and languages
Through all the generations
Of those who believed in Jesus
And His Holy Spirit.

And so it comes to us today.
The Bishops, successors of the Apostles,
Lay hands over us and anoint us with oil,
The signs of the coming down of the Spirit upon us.
They pray together with the whole community
That we be given the gifts of the Holy Spirit.

This is so that we, too,
Can go out to do Jesus' works
Just as the first Apostles did,
With great faith, courage, and power.
This is to fulfill what Jesus promised:

"I tell you most solemnly,
Whoever believes in me
Will perform the same works as I do myself,
He will perform even greater works,
Because I am going to the Father." John 14:12

* * * * * *

There is much more
That could be written
About the Spirit of God
And the hope He places in us
Through the Sacrament of Confirmation.
But let us end here for now.

8. A Note on Confirmation: Its History in the Church

How Did It Get Started?

In the early days of the Church the laying on of hands by the Bishop and the reception of the Holy Spirit were closely connected with the bath of Baptism. During the second through the fifth centuries, because the Bishop could not attend all of the baptismal services, the anointing ceremony of Confirmation was made into a separate ceremony and done when the Bishop could be present.

How Did the Meaning of Confirmation Change and Grow?

In some places, during the Middle Ages, confirmation of infants took place right after their Baptism, but as time passed on, Confirmation began to be generally reserved for older children and young adults. Confirmation was no longer viewed as part of the baptismal ceremony, but rather as a sacrament of personal growth, strengthening, and commitment. Young adults were given a tap on the cheek by the Bishop as a sign they should be ready to suffer for their faith in Jesus.

How Do Church Leaders Look at Confirmation Today?

Today the meaning of Confirmation is still being discussed and studied. Certainly it is closely connected in meaning with Baptism and the Eucharist as a sacrament of full entrance into the Christian community. In the Eastern Tradition, Baptism, Confirmation, and Eucharist are all given together, even to the infant coming into the Church.

9. Praying the Rosary

The Rosary

The Rosary is a meditation prayer to our Lord Jesus,
To our Father in Heaven,
And to the Holy Spirit.
It is also a special prayer to Mary,
The Mother of Jesus,
Asking for her guidance, protection, and help.
The Rosary has been a treasured prayer of the Church
For hundreds of years.

The Prayers of the Rosary

The Sign of the Cross

In the name of the Father,
+ and of the Son,
And of the Holy Spirit.
Amen.

The Apostles' Creed

I BELIEVE in God, the Father Almighty,
Creator of heaven and earth;
And in Jesus Christ, His only Son,
Our Lord; who was conceived by
The Holy Spirit, born of the Virgin Mary,
Suffered under Pontius Pilate,
Was crucified; died, and was buried.

He descended to the dead,
On the third day He arose again;
He ascended into heaven,
And sits at the right hand of God,
The Father Almighty; from thence
He shall come to judge the living and
The dead. I believe in the Holy Spirit,
The Holy Catholic Church, the communion

Of Saints, the forgiveness of sins, the
Resurrection of the body, and life everlasting.
Amen.

The Our Father

OUR FATHER, who art in heaven, hallowed
Be Thy name: Thy Kingdom come: Thy will be
Done on earth as it is in heaven. Give us
This day our daily bread: and forgive us our
Trespasses as we forgive those who trespass
Against us. And lead us not into temptation:
But deliver us from evil.
Amen.

The Hail Mary

HAIL MARY, full of grace; the Lord is with
Thee: blessed art thou among women, and
Blessed is the fruit of thy womb, Jesus.
Holy Mary, Mother of God, pray for us sinners,
Now and at the hour of our death.
Amen.

Glory Be to The Father

Glory be to the Father, and to the Son,
And to the Holy Spirit; as it was in the
Beginning, is now, and ever shall be,
World without end.
Amen.

The Hail, Holy Queen

Hail, holy Queen, Mother of Mercy! our life,
Our sweetness, and our hope! To thee do we
Cry, poor banished children of Eve; to thee do
We send up our sighs, mourning and weeping
In this valley of tears. Turn, then, most
Gracious advocate, thine eyes of mercy toward
Us; and after this our exile show unto us the
Blessed fruit of thy womb, Jesus; O clement,

O loving, O sweet Virgin Mary.
V. Pray for us, O holy Mother of God.
R. That we may be made worthy of the
Promises of Christ.

The Mysteries of the Rosary

The Joyful Mysteries

1st: The Annunciation
The Angel Gabriel appears to Mary,
Announcing that she is to be the Mother of God.

2nd: The Visitation
Elizabeth greets Mary:
"Blessed art thou among women
And blessed is the fruit of thy womb!"

3rd: The Nativity
The Virgin Mary gives birth
To the Redeemer of the world.

4th: The Presentation
Mary and Joseph present the child Jesus
In the temple.

5th: The Finding in the Temple
Mary and Joseph find Jesus in the temple.

The Sorrowful Mysteries

1st: The Agony in the Garden
At Gethsemane Jesus prays, and sweats blood
As He feels the weight of the sins of the world.

2nd: The Scourging at the Pillar
Jesus is cruelly whipped
Until His body can bear no more.

3rd: Crowning With Thorns
A crown of thorns is placed on the head of Jesus.

4th: The Carrying of the Cross
Jesus carries the heavy cross upon His shoulders.

5th: The Crucifixion
Jesus is nailed to the Cross
And dies after three hours of Agony.

The Glorious Mysteries

1st: The Resurrection
        Jesus rises three days after His death.

2nd: The Ascension
        Jesus ascends into Heaven
        Forty days after His Resurrection.

3rd: Descent of the Holy Spirit
        The Holy Spirit descends upon the Apostles.

4th: The Assumption
        Mary is united with her Son in Heaven.

5th: The Coronation
        Our Lord crowns His mother
        As Queen of Heaven.

These are the fifteen Mysteries of the Rosary.
These Sacred Events of our Lord's Life
Are Life for us when we think about them,
Praying along on the beads.

Prayers We Say at Wakes, Between the Mysteries of the Rosary

Leader: Eternal rest grant to him, O Lord.
People: And let perpetual light shine upon him.
All: And may the souls of all the faithful departed,
           Through the mercy of God, rest in peace. Amen.

*   *   *   *   *   *

All: O My Jesus, forgive us our sins;
           Save us from the fires of hell.
           Lead all souls to heaven,
           Especially those who have most need
           Of Thy mercy.

How to Say the Rosary

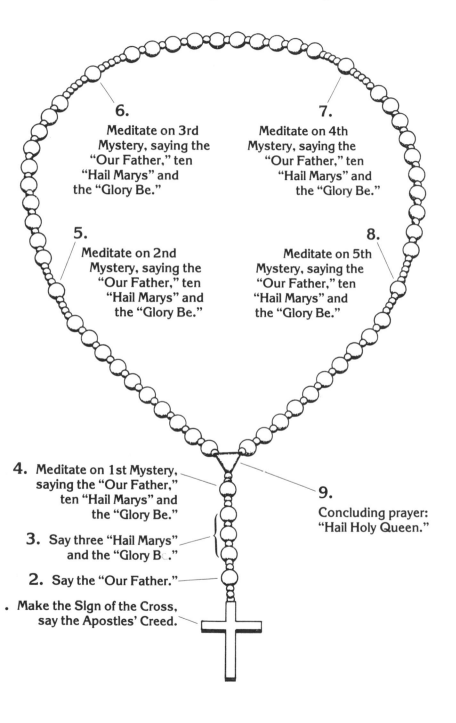

6. Meditate on 3rd Mystery, saying the "Our Father," ten "Hail Marys" and the "Glory Be."

7. Meditate on 4th Mystery, saying the "Our Father," ten "Hail Marys" and the "Glory Be."

5. Meditate on 2nd Mystery, saying the "Our Father," ten "Hail Marys" and the "Glory Be."

8. Meditate on 5th Mystery, saying the "Our Father," ten "Hail Marys" and the "Glory Be."

4. Meditate on 1st Mystery, saying the "Our Father," ten "Hail Marys" and the "Glory Be."

3. Say three "Hail Marys" and the "Glory Be."

2. Say the "Our Father."

. Make the Sign of the Cross, say the Apostles' Creed.

9. Concluding prayer: "Hail Holy Queen."

chapter five

THE MASS
THE EUCHARIST

*"Lord, I am not worthy to receive
You, but only say the word, and
I shall be healed."*

The Prayer before Communion from the Liturgy of the Eucharist

1. Indian Traditions That Relate in Meaning to Our Coming Together To Pray the Mass

What Did Eating a Meal Together Mean?

From the beginning,
Eating a meal together
Was an important part of the life of the People.
It was a holy event,
The coming together of the family,
The band, the tribe,
To share food and enjoy old friends.
It was a time for singing thanks
To the Creator for the gift of life.

"Feasting, sharing a meal with family and neighbors,
Was, in the earliest Indian way,
An act of thanksgiving.
In the ancestral manner, the People gathered
'To pray and pray' for the rebirth
Of another season, and the new gifts
Of roots and berries from the Divine Spirit." Clara Covington

There were Root Feasts in the Spring
And long songs and prayers of thanks
For the Earth's new gifts of food and medicine,
For the people's continued health and strength.
There were Berry Feasts in the Summer
In thanks for the Earth's first fruits
That grew in abundance on the forested slopes.

"Following the introduction of the Catholic Way,
The sharing in native feasting began to change.
Anglo holidays were introduced
Along with the festive Holy Days of Obligation,
Arresting the growth of the earlier traditions." Clara Covington

During Winter Dances,
When Powers were confirmed and renewed,
The meal was an occasion
For continuing prayer,
For giving thanks to the Creator for
Water and all good foods from the Earth.

When there was a death,
And relatives and friends from the other bands
Came to make a large gathering,
The meals were a sacred part
Of the prayer of the People
During the days of mourning.
The meal,
Made possible by the skills of hunters
And cooks, brought the People together in helping
The one passing on and the sorrowing family.

The meal began and ended in prayer
Bringing joy, strength, and peace
To the People. It helped to build
A union of hearts.
There was always food
For visitors to take home.

"In the earliest Indian way of life,
A death in the family
Was an occasion for a spiritual gathering,
A retreat from all earthly obligations.
Each neighbor, friend, relative, attended
In a respectful manner.
There was a great deal of silence
Along with prayers and speeches of sympathy.
Elders reminded everyone
To honor the food like a prayer." Clara Covington

How Was the Unexpected Guest Received?

The stranger, the traveler,
Was never allowed to stay hungry.
And when he moved on
He was given careful instructions
Where to find the food his hosts had cached
For visitors like him
Along the path of his journey.

What Were Earlier Catholic Indian Ways
Concerning the Sacred Meal, the Mass?

*"When the Indian people first accepted the Church
And all its teaching, it was accepted
That the blessed host was the spiritual food
For each who received.
This was true even though
It was difficult to interpret into Indian
The exact spiritual meaning of the Holy Communion.*

*In the earliest Catholic way
The Mass was in Latin.
The old people saw in the movements
Of the priest before the altar,
The passing of Jesus' life like a story.*

*The people said prayers and sometimes a rosary
In Indian before the Mass began,
And during Mass, sang many Indian hymns.
The priest heard confessions before Mass
And gave his sermon, both in the native tongue.*

*For some members the changes brought about
By the Second Vatican Council
Have been difficult to adjust to.
Change is hard to understand,
Especially when you were taught
That there would be no change."* Clara Covington

118

2. Some Indian Christian Ways of Looking at the Mass, the Eucharist

How Is the Mass Part of Our Journey Towards Our Creator?

We are all a People
Making a journey towards our Creator.
His Spirit gives us life
And calls us together at times
To pray for strength
For our journey.

"Praying by ourselves is necessary,
But when many pray together,
The voice is strong." Frank Halfmoon

The whole world is the Creator's house.
We walk in His Presence
Every day. The church our grandparents
Helped to build is small
But like the Creator's larger house;
We enter it to pray.

The Liturgy of the Eucharist, the Mass,
Is a long Prayer.
It is also a meal, a special meal in which
We give thanks to our Creator, Our Father,
Together with Jesus, Our Lord.

We give thanks for being allowed to participate
In all the mystery and beauty of life
Here on this good earth.
We give thanks for the joy of family,
Children, grandparents,
For the strength, goodness, hope
Placed in our hearts by the Holy Spirit.

For this meal
Jesus is the Host who invites us.
He is the Food we receive for our journey.
His loving Presence is the reason
For the peace and union we feel between us,
The joy we wish to pass on to others.
We bring what we can, ourselves:
We come to pray, to prepare the church,
To lead songs, to read, to assist the priest
At the altar, to take up the collection,
To make a People feel welcome and comfortable.

How Do We Begin Our Eucharistic Liturgy, The People's Work of Worship?

When the Mass begins
In the Name of the Father, Son, and Spirit,
We enter deeply into our Creator's Presence,
Preparing ourselves for Communion
With Our Risen Lord.
We ask, together, forgiveness
For our sins
Thinking how wonderful it is that
Jesus welcomes us kindly,
Just as we are,
All sinners.
"Lord have mercy."
"Glory to God in the highest . . ."

What Do We Do at the Readings?

We listen carefully to our Maker
Teaching, guiding, encouraging us
Through the Readings from the Bible
And through the words of the Speakers.
"Thanks be to God."
"Glory be to You, O Lord!"

We remember in words those
We especially want our People to pray for.
"Lord, hear our prayer."
We reaffirm the Faith we share.
"We believe in God . . ."

How Do We Pray During the Preparation of Gifts And During the Prayer of Thanks?

We bring forward and prepare the bread and wine,
Praising God, our Creator,
For the Beauty of His creation,
For all that He has given us.
"Blessed be God forever!"

We make a special prayer of thanks
To God for all He has done for us throughout
History to this day.
We call Him: "Holy, Holy, Holy . . ."

What Is the Prayer We Say to Announce Jesus' Coming Among Us in a Special Way?

We are all part of Jesus, The Priest,
Offering Himself to God, our Father, in thanksgiving.
The priest taking the bread
Says the words for us
Of Jesus to His disciples
At their last supper together:
"Take this, all of you, and eat it:
This is my body which will be given up for you."
Then, taking the cup;
"Take this, all of you, and drink from it:
This is the cup of my blood,
The blood of the new and everlasting covenant.
It will be shed for you and for all men
So that sins may be forgiven.
Do this in memory of me."

Jesus' great Love for us,
The total gift of His Life for us,
Becomes present among us
In a special way through the appearance
Of bread and wine.

Our Creator, our Father, accepts us
And our Prayer,
One with His Risen Son.
He loves us; He forgives us.
We wish to proclaim our Faith:
"Christ has died. Christ is Risen.
Christ will come again!"

What Do We Pray for Ourselves and the Whole World Around Us?

We ask the gift of His Spirit
For us, for the whole Church,
For all those seeking God.
We remember our grandparents
And all those who have gone before us.
We affirm the beauty,
The holiness,
The goodness,
The unity of all creation
In Jesus.
We say: "Yes! Amen!"

Together we say the Our Father.
We address our Father in heaven.
We ask that He be held Holy.
We ask that He fully shine through our world,
That our wills may be fully one with His
On this earth.
We ask for His Presence, Guidance, Strength,
To sustain us this very day.
We plead for the grace
To accept forgiveness.

We ask to be given the power to forgive.
We ask that He will lead us away from temptation
And free us from the power of Evil
Which threatens to overtake us.

Together we pray
That the deep Peace within us
Will go out from us
To all those around us
And to every living being.

How Do We Share Union With Each Other And With Our Lord?

The one bread is broken
And shared;
We receive our Lord Jesus
In the appearance of bread and wine.
We make our prayer of thanks,
Inviting our Lord into our hearts
To change them
And make them more like His own.

Going out of church together,
We wish one another
Christ's peace and goodness, hoping
To share what we have been given
With our families and everyone we meet.

We carry this Great Prayer,
The Mass, within us,
That if we have lived and died with Jesus
We will, also, live with Him forever.

The Mass is the death and resurrection of our Lord
Made present in and among us.
When we pray and live the Mass,
It becomes our death and resurrection
Together with Him.
The Love of our Lord poured out and into us

Is what rescues us from the death of sin
And fills us with strength, courage, and peace.
Jesus fills us with Himself, His saving Presence,
His Spirit,
And this is the ground of our hope
For eternal Life with Him.

3. Where Did This Great Prayer Of Thanksgiving and Sacrifice Come From?

How Did We Come to Have the Mass? Was There a First Mass?

Jesus enjoyed eating with His People.
As He journeyed around
He would often invite Himself to dinner,
Especially to dinner in the homes of those
Considered sinners or outcasts.

Meals were also traditionally sacred times
For Jesus' People.
For the Jewish People, sacred meals
Were occasions for prayers of pleading,
Thanksgiving, praise, and sacrifice.
They prayed for the Creator's help
And continued companionship
During their difficult life's journey.

Our Mass began
At the Last Supper
Of Jesus and His disciples.
Jesus, knowing that the time
Of His death was near,
Called His disciples together
To celebrate the Feast of the Passover.
The Passover was a sacred meal of thanks,

Reliving the Creator's deliverance
Of the Jewish people from slavery in Egypt.

When Moses was arguing with the Pharaoh,
The king of Egypt, trying to convince him
To let the Jewish People go free,
The Creator directed that the blood
Of a sacrificed lamb be smeared
Over the doorways of the Jewish homes.
During the night, Death "passed over"
The firstborn of the Jews
And struck the firstborn of the Egyptians.
This caused Pharaoh to let
Moses lead his People free.

The Pharaoh changed his mind
And pursued Jesus' ancestors to the
Banks of the Red Sea.
Through the Creator's help
The Jewish people passed safely through the sea
And away from their enemies.
They then, under Moses' leadership, journeyed forty years
In the desert before reaching
Their true home, the Promised Land.

During this Passover meal, celebrating
God's lasting agreement with His People
To love them and be with them forever,
Jesus did something wonderful.

Looking into the Mystery
Of this last meal He was sharing
With His friends,
Jesus realized that it was His Father's will
For Him to give up His life for the life
Of His friends.

He acknowledged His great love for His Father,
The Holy One of His People,
By giving thanks and offering Himself totally
To whatever was asked of Him.

"And being as all men are,
He was humbler yet,
Even to accepting death,
Death on a cross." Ph. 2:8

He was obedient.

He was full of terror,
Seeing what His death would cost,
Yet He bowed in respect to His Father.
He wished to acknowledge trust
In His Father's Love,
Trust in the mysterious way,
Through His suffering and death,
That His Father wished to rescue the world
From the powers of sin and darkness.

Torn to pieces with the fear of pain
And the fear of being abandoned, left alone,
He was like a lamb being led to slaughter.
Yet He strove to give His heart totally,
Clearly, thankfully, trusting His Father
Till the end.

"And as they were eating he took some bread,
And when he had said the blessing he broke it
And gave it to them.
'Take it,' He said, 'this is my body.'
Then he took a cup, and when he had returned thanks
He gave it to them, and all drank from it,
And He said to them,
'This is my blood, the blood of the covenant,
Which is to be poured out for many'." Mk. 14:22-25

Jesus, the Lamb of God
Pours out His blood for us
Through His death on the cross
To free us from slavery to sin and death.
He dies for us to guide and sustain us
On our journey to our true home, heaven.

Jesus helps us to pass over
From death to eternal Life.

Jesus knew He was leaving this life,
But He also wanted to remain
With those He loved.
And so He began this way
Of remaining with us forever
In an everlasting bond of friendship
And mutual trust.

Earlier, when they were walking
The roads of Galilee, Jesus told His followers:

"I am the bread of life...
If you do not eat the flesh of the Son of Man
And drink His blood,
You will not have life in you.
Anyone who does eat my flesh and drink my blood,
Has eternal life,
And I shall raise him up on the last day." Jn. 6:35, 53-54

At the Last Supper Jesus showed His disciples
The way He would continue to give
His Life to them forever.

After Jesus' death and resurrection
And the Gift of His Holy Spirit,
The disciples of Jesus
Continued gathering together for this memorial meal
To share Communion with the Risen Lord.
They "recognized Him at the breaking
Of the bread." Luke 24:35

How Did the Mass Come Down to Us Through the Ages?

And so it spread throughout the world,
This sacred meal of union with Our Lord

Present with us, offering with us,
Our lives and His to our Father.

Down through the centuries
The Mass has taken on many shapes and forms;
It has been prayed
In hundreds of languages.
But it has always remained this
Sacred meal of thanks and sacrifice,
The enduring Presence of Christ among us
In the total gift of His Heart in friendship:
Loving us, forgiving us,
Giving His life for ours,
Teaching us, strengthening us,
Unifying us, helping us
On our journey toward God Our Father.

"I am the living bread
Which has come down from heaven.
Anyone who eats this bread will live forever;
And the bread that I shall give
Is my flesh, for the life of the world." John 6:51

4. The Meaning of the Words: Mass, Eucharist, Tabernacle, Benediction, Corpus Christi

Mass

The word *Mass* comes from the Latin word
Missa. It means "sent."
It was first used to tell Catechumens
(Those being instructed for entrance into the Church)
To leave, before the faithful's full celebration
Of union and Communion with our Lord.

Missa gradually came to be used as a word

Meaning the Church's whole commemorative prayer
Of our Lord's Last Supper.
From the word *Missa* we have the word in English,
Mass.

Eucharist

The word *Eucharist* is another word we use
To name the Prayer we commonly call the Mass.
We speak of celebrating the Eucharist
Just as we speak of the celebration of the Mass.
The word *Eucharist* is taken from a Greek word.
It means "to give thanks."

The word *Eucharist* can also mean
Jesus Present through the appearance of the Bread
Blessed at Mass.
The Eucharist is, then,
The strong Presence of Jesus in our world—
Hidden, silent, yet the Presence
Of a Love greater than any other force or power.
Only when we are loved
Do we dare to love
And become more really who we are and can be.
This is why we keep Jesus
The Center of everything we feel is real and valuable,
Present through the Blessed Bread
In the Tabernacle of the Church.

Tabernacle

Tabernacle means "house," "dwelling place,"
Or "tent" where we keep the Blessed Bread or Hosts.
We can visit our Lord there,
And, kneeling in the silence of the church,
Reveal our hearts to Him.
It is from the tabernacle
That the priest or his helpers take Holy Communion
To bring to the sick.

Benediction

For Benediction or Blessing
The priest takes a large Host
From the tabernacle, placing it
In a large gold holder
Which shows forth the Host
Like the center of the sun.
He then blesses all the People
With Jesus present through the Eucharist.
The Host, placed in this way,
Shows how we see Jesus
Present through the Eucharist
As the Center of our being and our strength;
Jesus, God's great Love and Power
Coming towards us.

Corpus Christi

The Latin words *Corpus Christi* mean
"Body of Christ."
We carry the Eucharist
Through the streets of our towns
To special shrines families have built,
Asking Jesus' blessing
For each of our Reservation communities.

Walking along together,
Praying and singing,
We show we are happy that
Jesus lives among us
As His own People.

We are grateful for His Gift,
Himself, His Body and Blood,
Real food for our journey together
Toward eternal Life.

5. Some of the Other Things We See, and Feel, and Hear at Mass

Incense: What Does It Mean?

Often incense is used at Mass.
The burning charcoal is the sign of love
Placed in our hearts by the Holy Spirit.
The fragrant smoke rising up
And spreading out to all the People,
Is a sign of our prayer going up toward our Maker
And outward toward those worshipping with us.
The smoke purifies, blesses, and makes holy
The People and the sacred things and places.
In older Indian traditions
Sweet grass, tobacco, or dried cedar
Placed on smoldering bark
Made a wonderful smoke
For praying and blessing.

Holy Water: What Is It Used for?

Holy Water is used to purify, to cleanse,
To bless and make holy.
When used at Mass
It reminds us of our Baptism
And of our Creator's mercy towards us.
Holy Water is a prayer
For the protection, the health, and the well-being
Of our families and our homes.

Candles: What Are They the Sign of?

Candles burning are the sign
Of the Presence of Jesus.
They are the sign
Of our People praying.

The sanctuary light, always burning,
Tells us Jesus is present,
Through the appearance of bread,
In the tabernacle.
The candles on the altar
Tell us the Great Prayer,
The Mass, is being offered.
The tall Paschal Candle announces our hope:
Jesus, crucified, and risen from the dead!
The small votive candles
At the side of the church
Are lit when someone wants to make
A special prayer of thanks or request
To our Creator through His Saints.

Bells: What Does the Sound of Bells Tell Us?

The large church bell
Reminds us of the Presence of our Creator
At the center of our lives. The bell
Calls us to prayer.
The smaller bells at Mass
Tell us Jesus is present among us.
They encourage us to remain alert,
To join our People at prayer.
The sound of a bell
Is itself a prayer, a healing sound,
A voice for the Creator in us
And in our world.

Vestments: What Do They Mean to Say?

The clothes worn at Mass
Go back a long time.
The *white robes*
Are a sign of a person's Baptism.
They are a sign of dedication,
Of a desire for wholeness
And pureness of heart.

The *stole*
Worn over the shoulder by the Deacon
And over both shoulders by the Priest,
Is the sign of the Presence
Of Christ's saving power
At work in the Sacraments.
The Acolytes wear *scapulars*
Over their shoulders
As the sign of their role
In helping the People at prayer.

Colors: What Does Each Color Mean?

During the year
Different colors are worn at Mass.

Purple

Is the sign
Of our sorrow for sin
And of our turning to our Father,
In the midst of whatever suffering,
Sacrifice, and death our lives ask of us.
It is the color we wear at Wakes.
Purple is worn in Advent,
The time of our preparation for Christmas,
And during Lent,
The time of our preparation for Easter.

White

Is worn during Christmas time
And Easter time.
It is the sign of our joy
At the coming of our Creator into the world
As one of us. It is the sign of our Faith
In Jesus' resurrection from the dead
Into eternal life. White is, then,
The color of the Funeral Mass.
White is, also, the sign for a pure heart
And is worn on all Feasts of Our Lady.
White is the color for marriage.

Green

Is the sign of our hope.
Green is worn during the time we call "Ordinary Time."
This time is after Christmas
And after the Feast of the Gift
Of the Holy Spirit, Pentecost.

Red

The sign of the fire
Of love, is worn on Pentecost Sunday
To celebrate Jesus' gift of His Spirit to us,
And for all Masses in honor of the Holy Spirit.
Red is, also, the sign for the giving up
Of one's life for one's friends.
It is worn during Masses remembering
Our Lord's suffering and death
And on the Feast days of Apostles and Martyrs.

Gestures: How Do We Show How We Feel at Mass?

When we stand, it is in a spirit of respect
And freedom as our Creator's sons and daughters.
When we sit,
It is to listen carefully and learn.
We kneel in reverence
For the Creator's Presence among us
And because we feel sorrow for our sins.
We bow
To express our respect for our Maker
And for each other.
We embrace or shake hands
To express our unity.
The priest opens and raises his hands
To thank and praise our Father
And to ask for His help.

Music: Why Do We Have Music?

Music is meant
To express the People's heart.
There always has been music at Mass:
Psalms and hymns and sacred chants.
We are encouraged today
To sing songs which are a joy to us
And part of our own cultural heritage.

*   *   *   *   *   *

There is much more that could be written
About Christ's wonderful Presence
Among us in the Eucharist.
Let us end here for now.

6. A Note on the History of the Eucharist in the Church

When Was the First Mass?

Jesus first shared His life with His apostles through bread and wine during their last Passover Supper together. This holy meal celebrated God's faithfulness to His people, His saving them from slavery in Egypt. Jesus established a new relationship between Creator and humankind, and between one person and another, when He enabled His disciples to share His continuing Presence among them through the appearance of the bread and wine.

How Did the First Christian Communities Offer the Mass?

During the first hundred years after Jesus' death and resurrection, communities of His followers met in homes for a meal together. During the meal, together with readings, spontaneous prayers, songs, and teachings, Jesus' words were said over the bread and wine. Sharing the consecrated bread and wine, the

135

early Christians experienced and expressed their new relationship to God and to each other through the Risen Jesus' saving Presence among them.

Was the Mass Always Prayed in Churches and in Latin?

For the next two centuries Mass was still celebrated at home. The Eucharist (a Greek word which means to give thanks) was received in the hand and sometimes taken home to be given to the sick or for Communion during the week. During the following three centuries, when the persecution of the Christians stopped, they came out from underground and needed larger buildings for Mass. Prayers became more formal, and Pope Damasus asked that the language of the Mass be changed from Greek to Latin, the language of the people.

Was the Mass Always Prayed in a Very Formal Way?

From the sixth century until the twentieth century, the Mass became more and more formalized. The distance between the people and the clergy widened a great deal. The difference between priest and layman was emphasized. Mass became a holy event watched from a distance, a time for adoration of Jesus present in the Host. Many felt it was improper to go to Communion very often because of man's sinful nature. In reaction to this feeling about being human, Bishops told the people they must go to Communion at least once a year. The reading of the Bible was shied away from because the other Christian Churches stressed it so strongly.

How Do We Approach Our Great Prayer, the Mass, Today?

During our own times, especially since 1962 and the Second Vatican Council, the Pope and Bishops have urged that the Mass be in the language of the people, so that the people can participate more in the Mass. They also have encouraged frequent Communion, sometimes with both bread and wine, and more reading and explanation of the Bible. The priest now faces the people to show his unity with them. Spontaneous prayers were encouraged at the Prayer of the Faithful, and the Kiss of

Peace was meant to express the genuine love and respect of all the members of the community for each other.

Going back to two practices in the early Church, the Pope and Bishops felt that Communion could be received as reverently in the hand as on the tongue. Also, each community was encouraged to select men and women from the community to help bring Communion to the sick and shut-ins.

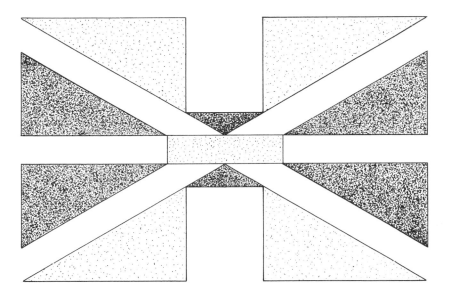

chapter six

RECONCILIATION

"God, the father of mercies,
Through the death and resurrection of His Son
Has reconciled the world to Himself
And sent the Holy Spirit among us
For the forgiveness of sins;
Through the ministry of the Church
May God give you pardon and peace,
And I absolve you from your sins
In the name of the Father, and of the Son,
And of the Holy Spirit."

"Amen."

The Prayer of Forgiveness from the Rite of Reconciliation

1. Indian Traditions That Relate In Meaning to the Sacrament Of Reconciliation.

How Did the People Live in Relation To the Creator and to Each Other?

From old times the People
Lived lives that were simple,
Unpretentious, honest, and generous.
They wanted to have a right heart
Toward everyone and all living things,
As much as possible.
There were many who lived flawless,
Impeccable lives of great purpose and dignity.
They were kind and generous men and women,
Filled with tremendous faith in their Creator
And full of knowledge of His Ways in our world.

They made prayers of thanks
To the Maker in the morning,
Praying in the Sweathouse, to the Grandfathers
To have mercy on them, to help them,
To give them peace, harmony, strength
For all the tasks of the day.
After bathing in the cold stream,
They stood before the sun,
Their hearts, their bodies pure and holy.

How Was Coyote a Part of This?

Coyote, too, was present
At work on the world
And among the People—
Coyote, a Force for good,
Coyote, the Player of tricks,
The creator of confusion;

Coyote, power for healing and laughter,
Coyote the Troublemaker;
Coyote, the mirror of human pride and foolishness.

"Coyote was the teacher of balance;
Coyote was a symbol of power." Michael Paul

Were There Strict Ways of Living?

There were strict laws of living
Within each band and tribe.
The survival of the whole People
Depended on the following of these laws.

"There were certain things
That both men and women did daily.
Each had tasks for teaching,
Each had tasks for living,
Each had tasks to the Creator,
Each had tasks to see that
Nature stayed in harmony,
Each had tasks for each other." Michael Paul

Children or adults did not do
Just as they pleased.
Children were taught respect
For themselves and their Elders
And for all living beings and things.
They were taught how to get along
And how they could contribute
To the life of the whole People.

Young people were taught to walk
Always in the Holy Presence,
Sharing whatever they had
With their family and the tribe.
They were taught to be kind
And hospitable to the stranger
And to take care of the old people.

Marriage bonds were respected.
Young girls were honored by the men
And protected by their grandmothers.
It was they, the women, who would bring
New life into the world.

If the strict ways of living
Were broken by a member of the band or tribe,
Punishment could be severe for adults:
A whipping and another chance
To live the ways of the People,
Or Banishment.

The Chief could also order
That the one who hurt others by his misdeeds
Give suitable gifts
To the family hurt by his actions;
This would be in recompense for
What they had lost,
Restoring a natural balance
And good relations between families.

Children who were disobedient
To their grandparents
Could expect a painful visit
From the village Whipperman.

These were days of great discipline,
Days when everything had a meaning
And everything held together;
Mornings when the old people
Stood happily before the sun and saw clearly
The origin and purpose of all living things,
And evenings when the old people
Stood calmly before the cool wind,
And saw clearly on the wide horizon
The rhythmic destiny of all living beings,

"These were days
When all felt the magic
Of the Creator." Michael Paul

142

2. The Song of a Suffering People

What Have the Indian People Had to Suffer?

"The Creator covered the People
With a blanket of love
To protect them." Tootie Mason

From the beginning, the People
Have been given wonderful gifts!
Land, roots, medicines,
Deer, horses, birds,
Water, salmon, trout,
A sense of the Holy Presence
Above and in
Each other and all things.

The Earth was good, too. There was
Plenty of room to live
And move about freely.
The Indian knew how to live here.

With the endless coming
Of the White Man this
All became confused,
And gradually the Indian lost
Some of the old ways.

We shared in the White Man's
Emptiness and confusion.
We shared in his drunkenness.
Because of his greed
And lack of feeling,
We were forced together, many bands
And tribes, in an unnatural way
In a place too small for us.
We were deprived of our Chiefs.
We were deprived of our Elders'
Knowledge and languages.

143

We learned to hate and distrust
Ourselves and each other through assimilation.
We walked around alone and empty,
Without purpose for living.
We were told we were only in the way,
That we were not beautiful,
That we had no value,
That our ways were not good
And led nowhere.

"This propaganda came from the whiteman." Michael Paul

It is only now

*"Because of some of our Tribal Spirit powers
and our good religious leaders"* Michael Paul

That we are finding ourselves again.
We see we are a beautiful and unique People,
That our ways are good and
Point in the direction
All men and women hope to go.
We see we can make the right choices
And direct ourselves toward what is
True and lasting and good forever.

We learned from our Ancestors,
(The saints that have gone before us)
To love and respect the earth
To live and work in harmony with her,
Everything having its place.

We learned to love and respect
Our old people,
To learn from them
And care for them in our homes
Until they are ready
To go to the place of Light.

We learned to love and respect
Ourselves and each person we meet,
To listen to them, to study them

144

And search in our minds
To see their role in the world,
Their special purpose
For being here with us.

We learned to love and respect
The Animals, learning how to live
From them, receiving from them
Gifts for healing and harmony,
Powers that healed us
And drew us together
As close friends and family.
These gifts were ours,
They were made for us;
We shared them with all who needed them.

In the old times
It was not easy to live.
The winters were long and cold.
Everyone had to work hard
And do their part to share with those
Who needed food and a place to stay.
But the People lived, happy and proud,
For thousands and thousands of years.

There is a tomorrow for us:
It is rich and full of hope—
Our tomorrow is with the Creator.
We came from the Maker's Mind;
We are all going back to Him.
It is important that we help
Each other on the way.

In the old days the People
Found God easily.

"They called Him by a different name:
Creator, Great Spirit,
The Maker-Guardian of all." Clarence Woodcock

They knew everything was made
By Him. They depended
On Him for life.
They knew that He
Cared about them
For He was present to them in a
Special way as "Tupia",
Grandfather-Grandmother,
Full of concern for them.

Grandfather lived among them as Sweathouse;
There to help, to heal, to console;
There to give wisdom and guidance,
The heat of the Sweathouse
Was the warmth of his Heart
Warming, opening, their hearts.

They knew that spiritual power
Was in everything, even in the rocks
And pebbles and streams,
In all living creatures.

They prayed every day,
In the morning and in the evening,
Giving thanks for being alive,
For being able to participate,
To share in the movement of all life
From birth to death to Life.

That is why there was always drumming
And singing and dancing—
The People always
Had a prayer in their hearts
Which they wanted to show forth
And let free.
This was so they could be well
And happy, and all around them could
Be well and happy.

3. We All Walk Together

How Do All the Churches and Religions Come Together?

We all walk paths,
We of the different churches and religions:
Washat, Drum and Feather,
Catholic, Tribal, Shaker, Presbyterian,
Charismatic, Methodist, Pentecostal.
We all walk paths leading
Up to the Creator of all things.

Can We Get Along and Help One Another?

We have much to learn
From one another
And much to give one another:
(Friendship, love, strength)
Each encouraging the other
To be free, to believe strongly,
To follow his or her way proudly,
Full of faith and hope.

We have a long way to go,
Some of us, on our journeys.
We find the going better
When we respect one another's faith,
Encouraging and helping one another
To be fully the way
We hope to be.

Without each one's way of going
We all weaken and die.
Our minds darken
And we lose our way.
There is seldom
Any future for us when

We don't love and respect
One another.

*"Let our hope, faith, and charity
Fulfill us all."* Michael Paul

4. Some Indian Christian Meanings Of the Sacrament of Reconciliation

*"I have come so that you might have life
And have it more abundantly.*
Jn. 10:1

How Does our Creator Look Towards Us When We Turn Away From Him?

We always walk in the Presence
Of a Creator who loves us,
Whose only concern is to save us,
To make us whole and well.
He wants to console and heal us,
To help us know ourselves
And find the Peace that is deep within us.

When we have sinned,
When we have turned away from God,
When we have deeply hurt someone or ourselves,
When we have been self-centered, ungrateful,
When we have acted as if there were no Creator
And no one else around us,
Our Creator remains turned towards us.
He remains concerned about us, devoted to us,
Eager to make us well again.

In What Way Can We Experience
Our Creator's Forgiveness of Our Sins?

Our Creator's kind of love
Is beyond our comprehension.
If we begin to be troubled by our sins
And are deeply sorry,
The moment we turn to Him
And ask forgiveness
He has already forgiven us.
He always loves us first.
We can, also, express our sorrow
And ask His pardon for our sins
Together with our brothers and sisters
At the beginning of Mass.

If something we have done or didn't do
Weighs very heavily on us,
We can go to the Sacrament of Confession
Or Reconciliation.
In this Sacrament we place ourselves
In the Presence of our Creator, our kind Father,
Jesus, who loves us, and
The Spirit, who heals us.

We confess our failures, our shortcomings,
Our sins, in the presence of a priest.
The priest is there as a voice
For Jesus and the Christian community, His Church.
He is there to console us
And guide us, and assure us
Of His love for us
Just as we are—sinners—
Sinners who desire to begin again
A life that is pure and holy.

Nowadays, after we have talked about our sins
And read some words from Scripture,
The priest might ask if we wish
To pray with him for our healing.

Then he will say the prayer of forgiveness
And sometimes place his hands on our head,
Asking the Holy Spirit to come down upon us
To strengthen and console us,
To give us peace.

Are There Times Now When We Can Experience The Sacrament of Reconciliation Together?

Sometimes we go to the Sacrament of Reconciliation,
Together with our whole community.
There we can sing and pray together
And listen to our Creator's concern for us,
His trust in us, expressed
In the Bible stories and prayers.

After this we can go to the priests
For Confession alone. Or we can
Confess our sins to God
In the silence of our hearts,
And receive the prayer of forgiveness from Christ,
Through the priest,
As we stand together with all our People.

After we have sinned and asked for forgiveness,
Jesus depends greatly
On the Christian community around us
To welcome us back,
To encourage us,
And help us to be well.

Our Christian brothers and sisters
Help us when they
Make us feel at home,
Even when we have hurt them.

Why Is It That Jesus Forgives Me My Sins?

We begin again and again.
That is the way we are.
But we must remember
Even if we were to nail Jesus to a cross,
He would simply look upon us and love us.

When someone (a grandmother,
A mother, a father, a brother or sister,
A husband, a wife, a friend) truly loves us,
We can only hurt them;
We cannot make them stop loving us.
This is the kind of love
That can change us.

In examining my life
And confessing my sins,
I do not seek to wipe out
All sin from my life,
All my faults and failures,
So that when I become perfect,
God will have good reason
To love me. No!
He loves me first while I'm sinner,
Reaches out to me, a sinner,
Wishing me to simply know
That He loves me as I am,
That He accepts me,
And will be right with me while I am
Trying to be more truly myself,
More free,
More honest,
More fully alive.

5. How Did the Sacrament of Reconciliation or Confession Come Down to Us?

What Did Jesus Ask of His Followers?

Our Sacrament of Reconciliation,
Or Confession, goes back to the time
Of the great deeds of Jesus,
When He began His public life of healing.
From the very first times of His preaching
And teaching, Jesus asked His People to become
Sorry for their sins and turn to His Father
For a new way of living,
Full of grace and truth:

*"Repent, for the kingdom of heaven
Is close at hand."* Mt. 4:17

Jesus praised those who approached God
In a spirit of humility, like
The tax collector who prayed in the temple,

*"Not daring even to raise his eyes to heaven;
But he beat his breast and said,
'God, be merciful to me, a sinner'."* Lk. 18:13-14

Jesus asked a great deal of His followers.
He even told them:

*"You must therefore be perfect
Just as your heavenly Father is perfect."* Mt. 5:48

The Ten Commandments,
Given to His ancestors
Through the great prophet Moses,
Jesus summed up in two laws of love:

*"You must love the Lord your God
With all your heart, with all your soul,*

And with all your mind. This is the greatest
And the first commandment. The second resembles it:
You must love your neighbour as yourself." Mt. 22:37-40

How Did Jesus Ask Us to Regard
Our Fellow Human Beings?

Jesus added a new meaning
To the notion of neighbor when He taught:

"You have learned how it was said:
You must love your neighbor
And hate your enemy. But I say this to you:
Love your enemies and pray for those
Who persecute you; in this way
You will be sons of your Father in heaven,
For He causes His sun to rise
On bad men as well as good . . ." Mt. 5:43–46

He taught that the way
We regard and care for each other
Is the way we regard
And care for Him:

"I tell you solemnly,
Insofar as you did this to one
Of the least of these brothers of mine,
You did it to me." Mt. 25:40

How Did Jesus Describe Those Who Belonged
To Him?

In response to the world's desire
For wealth, praise,
Power, luxury, ease,
Jesus gave His own picture of what those
Who belonged to God were like:

"How happy are the poor in spirit;
Theirs is the kingdom of heaven.

Happy the gentle:
They shall have the earth for their heritage.
Happy those who mourn:
They shall be comforted.
Happy those who hunger and thirst for what is right:
They shall be satisfied.
Happy the merciful:
They shall have mercy shown them.
Happy the pure in heart:
They shall see God.
Happy the peacemakers:
They shall be called sons of God.
Happy those who are persecuted in the cause of right:
Theirs is the kingdom of heaven." Mt. 5:3-10

You could not find a teacher
With higher standards for us,
Yet, in the midst of calling us to freedom,
He remained most understanding
And compassionate.

How Did Jesus Feel About Sinners?

He loved sinners,
(Those rejected by the world)
And found His friends among them.

"I did not come to call the virtuous,
But sinners." Mt. 9:13

There was the woman caught in adultery.
After Jesus had shamed her accusers
He said:

"'Woman, where are they?
Has no one condemned you?'
'No one, sir' she replied.
'Neither do I condemn you,
Go away, and don't sin anymore'." Jn. 8:10-11

There was the prostitute
Who kissed Jesus' feet
And bathed them with her tears.
Of her Jesus said to His host, who had not honored Him:

"For this reason I tell you
That her sins, her many sins,
Must have been forgiven her,
Or she would not have shown such great love.
It is the man who is forgiven little
Who shows little love." Lk. 7:47

He chose for disciples people
Whom others regarded as sinful:

"As He was walking on He saw
Levi the son of Alphaeus, sitting
By the customs house, and he said to him,
'Follow me' ...When Jesus was at dinner
In his house, a number of tax collectors
And sinners were also sitting
At the table with Jesus and His disciples:
For there were many of them
Among His followers." Mk. 2:14-16

How Did Jesus See His Way of Forgiving Sins?

Jesus saw His forgiving
As a healing.
He tried to restore those who believed in Him
To a wholeness they had not dreamed possible.
Once when He was preaching in a crowded room,
Men lowered a paralytic towards Him
Through the ceiling. Touched by their faith,
Jesus said: "My child,
Your sins are forgiven."
This caused some of His critics
To question His power to forgive sins.
He answered them:

"But to prove to you
That the Son of Man has authority on earth
To forgive sins—he said to the paralytic—
I order you: get up,
Pick up your stretcher, and go off home.
And the man did just that." Mk. 2:5-12

Jesus came among us
To reconcile us with one another
And with our Creator.
He came to help us experience
A self-knowledge, a harmony,
A unity, a friendship, a peace
With our Father,
And with one another.

Did Jesus Teach Us to Judge Persons Or to Forgive Them?

He had a way of trying to
Bring people together.
He admonished His followers:

"Be compassionate as your
Father is compassionate." Lk. 6:36

He asked us not to judge each other harshly:

"Why do you observe the splinter
In your brother's eye and never notice
The plank that is in your own?...
Take the plank out of your own eye first,
And then you will see clearly enough
To take out the splinter
That is in your brother's eye." Lk. 6:41-42

When Peter asked Jesus:

"Lord, how often must I forgive my brother
If he wrongs me? As often as seven times?"

Jesus answered him, *"Not seven, I tell you,*
But seventy-seven times." Mt. 18:21-22

Jesus felt that love and forgiveness,
Reconciliation, were necessary
Before we could really pray:

"So then, if you are bringing your offering
To the altar and there remember
That your brother has something against you,
Leave your offering there before the altar.
Go and be reconciled with your brother first,
And then come back and present
Your offering." Mt. 5:23-25

Even when He was dying on the cross
Jesus prayed earnestly for those
Who were killing Him:

"They crucified Him there
And the two criminals also,
One on the right, the other on the left.
Jesus said, 'Father, forgive them;
They do not know what they are doing'." Lk. 23:33-34

How Did Jesus Pass On His Power
For Forgiving Sins to Us?

After His death and resurrection
Jesus appeared to His Apostles
And passed on to them
The power of forgiving sins.
He brought them peace.
He gave them His healing and forgiving Spirit:

" 'Peace be with you.
As the Father sent me,
So am I sending you.'
After saying this He breathed on them and said:
'Receive the Holy Spirit.
For those whose sins you forgive,
They are forgiven;

For those whose sins you retain,
They are retained'." Jn. 20:21-23

And so His apostles and their successors
Continued to be Jesus' forgiving,
Healing Presence in the world.
The apostles forgave sins
Through the power of the Holy Spirit
In the Name of Jesus, the Lord.

In different forms and languages,
Down through the centuries,
Christians have tried to forgive one another
And become reconciled with their Creator
And with one another
Whenever sin tore families, communities,
Countries, the world, apart.

St. Paul, who himself was cured
Of his blindness and reconciled to the Christian
Community by Christ through the Holy man, Ananias,
Felt that reconciliation was an essential part
Of the good news of Christ:

"In other words, God in Christ
Was reconciling the world to Himself,
Not holding men's faults against them,
And He has entrusted to us
The news that they are reconciled.
So we are ambassadors for Christ;
It is as though God were appealing through us,
And the appeal that we make in Christ's name is:
Be reconciled to God." 2 Cor. 5:19-21

The Bishops, the successors of the apostles,
And their helpers, the priests,
Continue their special role of reconciliation
In the Christian communities.
These men, chosen from the community
To be Jesus' special voice and hands
For the blessing of forgiveness,

Continue to assure their fellow Christians
Of the Creator's boundless love towards them
In Christ Jesus our Lord.

6. Some Questions We Might Ask Ourselves in Preparing for the Sacrament of Reconciliation

How Do I Stand Before My Creator, My Kind Father?

How do I stand
Before Jesus, His Son
With His great love for me?

How do I stand
In the Presence of the Holy Spirit?
Do I live a life guided
By the voice of my conscience,
The movement toward good
Of this Spirit in my heart?

How do I stand
Before Mary, my Mother,
Before Jesus, her Son,
Before God, my kind Father,
With the Spirit in my heart?
What can I say? What do I wish
To tell them?

Have I Sincerely Tried to Find My Creator, My Father, in My Life?

Do I walk in His Presence each day?
Do I thank Him for all
He gives to me? Do I see
How He is in me and all around me?

Am I patient with Him, with others,
With myself? Do I trust Him?
Do I love Him
And wish to know Him
And give my will over to His will?
Do I want to be with Him forever?

Like Jesus, Do I Love Others

As I love my own self?
Am I willing to make sacrifices
For my family, for my friends,
For my community?
Do I sincerely respect myself
And others, and all life
That shares this earth with me?

Have I Tried to Solve Differences

Between myself and my family,
Between myself and all those
I'm feuding with?
Can I forgive old wounds and insults,
And make peace with those who seem to hate me
Enough to
Even wish me gone?

Do I Take Special Care of the Young,

Both of my family and of other families?
Do I try to give them good example
And take time to be with them,
Encourage them, and help them
Find themselves?
Do I share my deepest values,
And hopes and beliefs with them
As they question and grow ready
To learn, to believe?

Do I Respect the Old and Care for

Their need to be noticed and heard,
And learned from; their need
For food and medicine, transportation,
Winter warmth and companionship;
Their need to remain
Actively part of the community?

Have I Brought What I Could of Strength, Vision, Joy and Hope to the Sick,

The forgotten, the shut-in?
Have I gone to the jails, to Juvenile,
Remembering, caring, being there,
Offering what little help I could?

Do I Share Whatever I Have

With my family, my friends, the needy,
The unexpected guest, the stranger?
Do I enjoy giving gifts
When I can, to show
My appreciation, my esteem, my love?

How Do I Show My Love, My Gratitude, To My Husband or Wife?

Am I faithful
In my married love, generous and kind?
Can my children and grandchildren
See the Creator's love in us?
Do I try to keep other couple's marriages
Sacred and strong?

How Patient Am I With Those
Who Have Been Drunk or Drugged?

How patient am I with the lonely,
The confused, the anxious, the depressed?
Do I have time for them?
Do I listen to them and remain with them
Even in their illness?

How Much Compassion Do I Feel

For others in their weaknesses:
For the run-arounds, the lost,
The homosexual, the lesbian,
Men and women desperately looking for love?

Do I Treat All Human Life as Sacred,

Working to create a community in which
No couple would want to have an abortion;
A community in which young women and men
Are honored,
And human sexuality is esteemed and enjoyed
Responsibly, in an atmosphere
Of genuine love and respect?

Do I Live In Harmony With the Earth,

Taking only what I need,
So that there will be as much food,
Fuel, and clothing as possible
For all the people in the world?

*　*　*　*　*　*

There is much more that could be written
About the Sacrament of Reconciliation
And the great strength, healing, and peace
That can come to us through the Presence
Of the Holy Spirit in the Church.
But let us end here for now.

7. A Note on Spirits and Powers

There are great powers from the
Holy Mystery: Father, Son, Spirit,
And from the angels and saints
Both on earth and in heaven.
There are great powers from the
Evil Mystery: Satan, thrown from heaven
And with his fallen angels
Let loose upon this earth.

We are given the powers
Of the Holy Mystery
To overcome the Evil One.
We believe Good is more powerful
Than Evil
And is overcoming it.

Powers given for doing good
(For healing hearts, minds, and bodies,
For influencing people to good)
Are powers from the Holy Spirit,
And from all in union with this Spirit.

Powers can be used to do evil:
To harm, to cripple, to kill.
These evil wishes come from jealousy,
Envy, bitter hatred, selfishness.
Powers used in these bad ways

Lead to death.
They are from the Evil One, Satan,
And from all in union with him.

When we really love someone
And care for that person,
The Holy Spirit is in us.
When we just use someone,
The Holy Spirit is not with us.

When we listen carefully to someone,
The Holy Spirit is with us.
If we cannot see or hear anyone else,
The Holy Spirit cannot yet fully make a home within us.

When we help someone who needs our help,
The Holy spirit is with us.

When we forgive someone
And wish even our enemies well,
The Holy Spirit is working within us.

It is the Holy Spirit's hope
To live within us and give us peace.
It is the Holy Spirit's desire
To bring healing and goodness into the world
Through us.

It is the hope of the Evil One
To possess us and fill us with anxiety and despair.
It is the desire of the Evil One
To bring sin, sickness, death into the world
Through us.

8. A Note on the Holy Spirit

The Holy Spirit
Is the Creator's gift to us
Of His own Love,
His own Life.
The Holy Spirit is active
In all of nature, giving life and growth
Through death.
Everything lives and dies
And lives again a new life.
The trees do, and the animals.
We, too, live and die
And live again, more full of life
Because of this Spirit given us.

Jesus, through His death,
Gave us His Spirit, His Power
For life and growth, for unity,
For truth, for good.
This Spirit in us is
Completely against the Power of Evil
Which causes emptiness, hatred,
Lies, and deceit.

This same Holy Spirit,
Active and alive in making
All that is good and lasting in our world,
Places a hope in us
That goes beyond our suffering,
Confusion, and despair;
A hope that goes beyond death.

This is the One
Who helped those who went before us.
This is the Spirit of Life and Goodness
Which Jesus gives us through His People
At Baptism and Confirmation.

This is the Spirit of Reconciliation,
Of light, and strength, and truth.
Nothing can overcome this Spirit,
Not even death.

Jesus said He had to leave us
So we could carry on His work
In the world. He sent His Holy Spirit
Upon us to work in and through us,
To help all beings on their journey
Toward our kind Father.

9. A Note on the History of The Sacrament of Reconciliation In the Church

Was the Sacrament of Penance or Confession Always the Same as We Know It Today?

In the first two hundred years or so after Jesus' death and resurrection, the early Christian communities believed that Baptism forgave a person's former sins. There are few indications of public Penance after Baptism. In some places there was no absolution for serious sin; the need for forgiveness was left to the judgment of the Creator.

During the third century the Church determined what sins could be forgiven. Penance was public. This was a once-in-a-lifetime event and was required if one gave up the Faith, committed murder, or was openly unfaithful to marriage vows.

From about the fourth to the tenth century, the Irish monks encouraged private Penance. They composed books with suggested penances for each sin. A person could be given Penance more than once. The question arose: Should Penance be a public or private event?

How Did the Sacrament of Confession Grow Into the Sacrament of Reconciliation?

From the twelfth century onwards, Penance became known as Confession and was to be in private. It was considered necessary to go to Confession at least once a year. Many people felt one had to go to Confession before going to Communion, even though the Church required this only in the case of serious sin.

In our own times the Rite of Penance, or Confession, has become the Sacrament of Reconciliation. Like the former rites, it includes sorrow for sins, confession, absolution, and firm purpose of amendment. But it also places a new emphasis on the healing of our relationship with Jesus, with ourself, with our community. The new rite stresses change of heart, a praying to Jesus through this Sacrament to really change our way of living. The new rite brings out more how happy and grateful and reborn we can feel when we are forgiven. Church leaders hope the new rite will help us understand ourselves better, and help us to better experience the healing of heart and mind and memories that Jesus can accomplish in us through the gift of His Holy Spirit in this Sacrament.

0. Prayers For Forgiveness

Lord, Jesus, I am sorry for hurting You
And Your brothers and sisters,
Who are so dear to You,
By what I have done or failed to do.
Please help me, Lord, to sin no more.

*　*　*　*　*　*

Lord Jesus, have mercy on me, a sinner.

chapter seven

THE ANOINTING
OF THE SICK

"Through this holy anointing
May the Lord in His love and mercy help you
With the grace of the Holy Spirit."

"Amen."

"May the Lord who frees you from sin
Save you and raise you up."

"Amen."

From the Rite for the Anointing of the Sick

1. Indian Traditions That Relate In Meaning to the Sacrament of the Anointing of the Sick

From olden times the power of healing
Has been a gift among the People.
This is the way the Creator took care of the Indian People.
There has always been someone in the band or tribe
To whom a sick person
Could go for help.
The sickness might be weakness,
Emptiness, loneliness of spirit,
Darkness and confusion of the mind,
Fear, anxiety, depression in the heart,
Or pain and disease in the body.
There was someone who could help.

They were wise men and women
Of deep personal prayer.
They knew the healing roots and plants
And the times for finding and using them.
They gathered these roots and plants
After prayer, with great respect
And gratitude.

They were men and women gifted
With a power for healing.
They worked on the one sick,
Using their hands or breath
Or sacred things, in silence or singing,
Encouraging the sick person
To sing her own healing song
So that she might be well again.

Before beginning to work
For the person asking to be healed,
The one praying for healing
Wanted to know whether the sick person

Was sincere in his faith
And really wanted to be made whole again.
It helped if the sick person wanted to be healed
For a good or generous purpose.
This knowledge and these powers for healing
Did not come to everybody
But just to certain individuals in the band or tribe.
If the persons to whom this power of healing
Was offered accepted this gift,
They then accepted a whole way of life.
It meant days of faithful prayer,
Sobriety, self-sacrifice, and complete
Dedication to their role of helping their People.
It was not an easy path to follow,
Nor is it an easy path today. Yet we
Still have men and women with these gifts
Who follow this Way today.
It is a great blessing to us.

2. Indian Christian Ways of Understanding the Sacrament of the Anointing of the Sick

What Is the Meaning of the Anointing With Holy Oil and the Laying On of Hands?

Since ancient times oil has been used
For cleaning, for healing,
For warmth and light.
Within Church traditions
The Anointing with sacred oil
Brings the sick person into close contact
With the saving Presence of our Creator.
Anointing with holy oil is the sign
Of the gift of wholeness and purpose.
From ancient times, too,

The laying on of hands has been
A prayerful way of passing on
The gift of warmth and healing,
And the blessing for peace and forgiveness.
In Church traditions
The laying on of hands is the sign
Of prayer for the gift of the Holy Spirit.
Within the Christian tradition
Birth, strengthening, and healing
Have always been important.
Through the Sacrament of the Anointing of the Sick
The person is healed for continuing life:
Here and now in the Church on earth,
Or forever with the Church in heaven.

Is the Anointing of the Sick Just for the Dying?

Within our communities the priest
Usually brought the oils for anointing
To help someone seriously sick
Or close to death. Because of this practice
Many people associated the Anointing of the Sick
Only with dying and death.
We call Confession, Anointing, Communion
When given to a seriously ill person,
The Last Rites.

Actually, the Anointing of the Sick
Is, like the other Sacraments, a prayer
Of the family and community together with Jesus,
For the full life and health of the sick person.
It is a prayer for the strength,
Wholeness, and holiness of the sick person
Here now on this earth if possible.
If the sick person's time to die has come,
The Anointing of the Sick is the family's
And community's prayer for the person's safe
Passing through death to eternal Life.

What Is This Prayer of Anointing Like?

In the face of both sickness and death
The anointing is a prayer together with Jesus
To our Creator, our kind Father,
Who may seem silent
Before the suffering of His son or daughter.

It is a prayer of trust
That He will come in power through the Holy Spirit
To restore the sick person to health,
Or raise the dying person from death to Life.

It is a strong prayer for
Faith, hope, and peace,
Both for the one lying down
And for all the family and friends standing round.

Often the priest will ask
Other prayerful persons present to help
By laying their hands, too,
On the sick person, praying
That Jesus will send
The deep peace
That He alone can give.

Who Can Receive This Anointing?

Encouraged by our Pope
And by the leaders of the Church,
It is appropriate today for us to give
The Sacrament of the Anointing of the Sick
Not only to those seriously ill,
But also to all the following:
The old,
Those about to undergo surgery,
Children who are sick but able to understand
The reason for the anointing,
Those suffering from mental or emotional sickness

But clear-minded enough to understand the prayer,
And those who, though now unconscious,
Would have wanted their fellow Christians'
Prayer of anointing.

Where Can This Prayer of Anointing Take Place?

This prayer of anointing
Can be done anywhere.
The family can gather together with the priest
At home, or around a hospital bed.
The whole community can gather
Together at a Sunday Mass to pray
For all those, young and old,
Desiring to be prayed for, anointed,
And healed by Christ our Lord.

What Is Our Hope Through This Prayer?

In all of our prayers
For the Anointing of the Sick,
We have this great faith in us
That Jesus is
The Presence of Love
Towards us
In our world. His Love is
Hidden, silent, yet the most
Powerful force in the world,
Greater than any other force or power
To change our hearts, minds, and bodies.

Jesus has these weapons:
A greater Presence,
A greater Wisdom,
A greater Love,
A greater Action
Than the Evil One.

Jesus outwits and overcomes our Enemy
Through our Faith
In His Love for us,
And through our hope
In His life-giving Spirit.

3. A Simple Blessing of Oil for Healing, The Blessing With Water, The Blessing of Medals and Rosaries

The Blessing of Oil for Healing

There is a beautiful prayer for healing
That can be done by a priest
Together with any devout group of Christians.
This prayer is for any of us
Who might become worried and confused,
Fall sick and lose our way.
Everyone gathers together
Comfortably in a room. All sit
Around a table with a candle, a crucifix,
Holy Water, a towel,
And a small container of a pure oil
Like olive oil,
Oil from growing things,
Oil with life in it.

Everyone places himself quietly
In the Presence of the Creator.
After some silence
There may be a reading from Scripture:
One of the stories about Jesus healing
Someone who asked for His help.
After this there can be more silent prayer
And a prayer of faith together, the Apostles' Creed.
Then the priest prays a prayer of blessing

For the oil, that it might become holy.
The priest blesses the oil with Holy Water.

After this, the person asking
To be prayed for may explain
What it is that he or she
Wants to be freed from through Jesus' power.

The priest and each person present
Then anoints the person
On the forehead and the hands,
With the sign of the cross.
If it is convenient
They may anoint the place on the body
Where sickness has a hold.
Each one, also, can lay his hands
On the sick person,
Praying in his own way
For health and healing.

After the prayer for healing,
All can stand and say an Our Father together,
Sing a song, and give each other
A sign of Peace.

What Are Some Other Simple Prayers We Use For Health and Healing?

It is good for us, too,
To sign ourselves with water that has been blessed
And to wear medals and carry rosaries in honor of Jesus,
Mary, and all the saints,
For our health and healing.

It is good to pray intently
Over a glass or cup of water
And give it to the sick person to drink
After he has told his wish for healing.

It is good to pray over medals and rosaries
Together with the priest,
Wishing good health and protection
For the one who wears or carries them.

In all of these things we show
That we remember our kind Father,
And that we trust the healing and protecting
Power of His Spirit,
Working through the simplest things
And through the prayers of His saints,
To save us and make us holy.

4. Our Way to Wholeness

> *"Jesus said to the paralytic, 'Courage, my*
> *Child, your sins are forgiven...get up,*
> *And pick up your bed and go off home'."*
>
> Mt. 9:2, 6 and 7

Most of us experience ourselves as incomplete,
Sometimes even torn in two.
As St. Paul says:

"I cannot understand my own behavior.
I fail to carry out the things I want to do,
And I find myself doing the very things I hate." Rm. 7:15-16

We desire to be free and kind persons;
Often we find ourselves selfish, hard, and cruel.

We desire to be open, loving, able to suffer for others;
We often find ourselves closed, angry, blaming
Others for our depression, frustration, emptiness.
We desire to feel whole, healthy, unified,
Full of creative energy for the good;
We often find ourselves broken, sick, confused,
With little or no energy for going forward
Or doing anything that truly gives life.

We desire to feel in harmony with our own being
And with all people and things on this good earth;
Yet we fail to rely totally on our Creator.

It is most important for us to want
To give up our life of sin.
If there is any lust, hatred, envy,
Jealousy, possessiveness within us,
We ask Jesus to help us to let it go,
To root it out from our heart
Where it suffocates us
And stunts our growth.

If there is anyone or anything we have hurt
And not asked for forgiveness;
If there is anyone who has hurt us
And we have not forgiven;
If there is any memory which frightens or hurts us,
That we have not placed honestly before Jesus
To be seen anew;
If there are any habits or feelings we cling to
Which lead us away from Him
And isolate us from those we love, then
It will be more difficult for Jesus to heal us.
We must be sincere and honest with Him.

Anything in us in which the Evil One
Can make a dwelling place must go,
Before Jesus and the Light of His Spirit
Can fully dwell in us
And shine out through us to others.
We often find ourselves hating ourselves,
Isolated from others, unable to see
What is good and lasting and beautiful around us.

We desire to trust totally in the Heart of our Lord
And in the hearts of our family and friends
Turned toward us in love and compassion;
But we are often so buried in the fog
Of our guilt and self-doubt
That we can't see the Sun breaking through.

We desire to reach out to others
But we are afraid they will ignore
Our eyes and hands.
We desire to be made well again
But we are afraid to ask our Lord,
Or to ask others to pray for us.
We are afraid that it won't make any difference,
That we aren't worthy even to ask
For such help and wholeness.

But we must trust Jesus
And those who pray to help us.
We must place our eyes on Him,
Place ourselves like children
In the loving hands of grandparents,
And ask that He have pity on us,
Rescue us, and change us.
It is like asking Him to sweep our house clean
So that He can more fully live there.

Only when Jesus has helped us to fully let go
Of everything that is not good and true,
Everything that is not of Him,
Only then can we hope to enjoy the Wholeness
Of His dwelling fully within us.
It is truly then we are re-created,
Born into a whole new person.

It is our Lord's desire to heal us
And bring us the fullness of life.

"I have come
So that they may have life
And have it to the full." Jn. 10:10

Jesus' greatest joy
Is a man or a woman most fully Alive!

5. To Do "Something Beautiful for God"

Mother Teresa

Jesus wishes to be Present,
To shine the light of His Healing Presence,
The Light of His Love, the Holy Spirit,
Through us, His Body on earth
To all those who are hurting in the world.

He needs our eyes to see,
Our ears to listen,
Our hands to touch and hold
Those who suffer, those with little or no hope,
His brothers and sisters.

They, too, are His Body;
He suffers in and with them.
When they hurt, when they die,
It is His hurting, His dying.

Most of us are far from being whole,
Far from being loving and free.
Most of us are wounded and broken,
And divided within ourselves.

Yet because of His great kindness to us,
There is this spark of Love, of Light
Within us. This spark burns within
And asks to be let out, to be shared.

Shattered, weak as we are,
He still makes His home within us
And wishes us to bring this little Light
Out to others.

We are totally unworthy of such a Gift,
Such a Treasure within us.
But this little Light, when shared,
Can become a Fire to change the earth,
A Fire meant one day
To merge with the Sun.

It is important for us,
Just as we are,
To bring our little Light,
(Our heart torn to pieces
With doubt and fear,
Our eyes blurred from weeping,
Our scarred hands) and reach out to touch
Those hurting as much as or more than we.

It is important for us all,
Imperfect as we are,
To join together in prayer
For our brothers and sisters caught
In the sea of pain we all are bathed in,
For our brothers and sisters caught
In the final darkness of dying that
We all find our way home in.

*" 'My soul is sorrowful to the point of death.
Wait here and keep awake with me.'
And going on a little further
He fell on his face and prayed."* Mt. 26:38-39

6. How Did the Sacrament of the Anointing of the Sick Come Down to Us?

Jesus Came to Heal Us.

Jesus came to heal us,
Not just from our sins,
But from sickness as well.
When John the Baptist sent out his disciples
To ask Jesus whether He was
The One they were waiting for, Jesus replied:

"Go back and tell John what you have seen
And heard: the blind see again,
The lame walk,
Lepers are cleansed,
And the deaf hear,
The dead are raised to life,
The Good News is proclaimed to the poor
And happy is the man who does not
Lose faith in me." Luke 7:22-23

During his public life Jesus worked hard,
Curing as many people as He could
Who had faith in Him.

"He sat there, and large crowds came to Him
Bringing the lame, the crippled, the blind,
The dumb and many others;
These they put down at His feet,
And He cured them.
The crowds were astonished to see
The dumb speaking, the crippled whole again,
The lame walking and the blind with their sight,
And they praised the God of Israel." Mt. 15:30-31

Jesus expressed surprise if someone
Did not think He wanted to cure him:

"A leper now came up and bowed low
In front of Him. 'Sir,' he said,
'If you want to, you can cure me.'
Jesus stretched out His hand,
Touched him and said,
'Of course I want to! Be cured!'
And his leprosy was cured at once." Mt. 8:1-3

Jesus wanted the sick person to tell Him
Exactly what he or she wanted Him to do:

"Then Jesus spoke, 'What do you
Want me to do for you?'
'Master,' the blind man said to Him,
'Master, let me see again.'

Jesus said to him,
'Go, your faith has saved you.'
And immediately his sight returned
And he followed Jesus along the road." Mark 10:51-52

Jesus' Ways of Healing

Jesus cured with His hands:

" . . . a woman was there who for eighteen years
Had been possessed by a spirit
That left her enfeebled;
She was bent double and quite unable
To stand upright. When Jesus saw her
He called her over and said,
'Woman, you are rid of your infirmity'
And he laid his hands on her.
At once she straightened up and she glorified
        God." Luke 13:11-13

Jesus cured with His hands and mouth:

"And they brought Him a deaf man
Who had an impediment in his speech;
And they asked Him to lay His hands on him.
Jesus took him aside in private,
Away from the crowd, put His fingers
Into the man's ears and touched his tongue
With spittle. Then looking up to heaven
He sighed; and he said to him,
'Ephphatha', that is, 'Be opened'.
And his ears were opened,
And the ligament of his tongue was loosened
And he spoke clearly." Mk. 7:32-35

Jesus cured using the earth:

" 'As long as I am in the world
I am the light of the world.'
Having said this, He spat on the ground,
Made a paste with the spittle,

183

Put this over the eyes of the blind man,
And said to him, 'Go and wash in the pool . . .'
So the blind man went off and washed himself,
And came away with his sight restored." Jn. 9:5-7

Jesus cured using just his voice:

"As He entered one of the villages,
Ten lepers came to meet Him.
They stood some way off and called to Him,
'Jesus! Master! Take pity on us.'
When He saw them He said,
'Go and show yourselves to the priests.'
Now as they were going away
They were cleansed." Lk. 17:12-15

Sometimes if someone just touched His clothing,
The person was healed:

"Then from behind Him came a woman,
Who had suffered from a hemorrhage for twelve years,
And she touched the fringe of His cloak,
For she said to herself,
'If I can only touch His cloak
I shall be well again.'
Jesus turned round and saw her;
And He said to her, 'Courage, my daughter,
Your faith has restored you to health.'
And from that moment
The woman was well again." Mt. 9:20-22

The Necessity of Faith

Jesus asked great faith of those
Who came to Him for healing.
He had great difficulty working
In His own home-town, Nazareth:

" . . . and He could work no miracle there,
Though He cured a few sick people
By laying His hands on them.
He was amazed at their lack of faith." Mt. 6:5-6

When there was great faith,
As in the case of the Roman soldier
Who wanted Jesus to save his favorite servant,
Jesus cured even from a distance:

"So Jesus went with them,
And was not very far from the house
When the centurion sent word to Him by
Some friends: 'Sir,' he said,
'Do not put yourself to trouble;
Because I am not worthy to have you
Under my roof; and for this same reason
I did not presume to come to you myself;
But give the word and let my servant
Be cured . . .' When Jesus heard these words
He was astonished at him and, turning round,
Said to the crowd following Him,
'I tell you, not even in Israel
Have I found faith like this!'
And when the messengers got back to the house
They found the servant in perfect health." Lk. 7:6-10

The Necessity of Prayer

Jesus believed strongly
In the power of prayer.
When His disciples were unable to help
A boy possessed by a devil,
Jesus commanded the unclean spirit to come out
Of the boy. Then He told His disciples:

"This is the kind . . .
That can only be driven out by prayer." Mk. 9:29

Often He went alone at night to the mountains
To pray when the multitudes were no longer
Pressing round Him to be helped.

185

The Way of Suffering

Jesus spoke of suffering,
That we should be ready to suffer
And bear our own cross:

"If anyone wants to be a follower of mine,
Let him renounce himself
And take up his cross and follow me." Mt. 16:24

In Matthew's vision of Him
Jesus took on our sicknesses
To free us from them:

"He cast out the spirits with a word
And cured all who were sick.
This was to fulfil the prophecy of Isaiah:
He took our sicknesses away
And carried our diseases for us!" Mt. 8:16-17

But when Jesus described the suffering
We would have as His followers,
It was not necessarily physical sickness
But the rejection, persecution, tiredness,
That can come to us when we try to stand up
For what we believe is true and good.

"Happy are you when people abuse you
And persecute you and speak all kinds of calumny
Against you on my account.
Rejoice and be glad, for your reward
Will be great in heaven; this is how
They persecuted the prophets before you." Mt. 5:11-12

Jesus cured all types of sickness:
Blindness, bleeding,
Paralysis, fever,
Even sickness unto death.
It seemed clearly His will to free
As many as He could from sickness
Of mind, body, and soul.
He was anxious to free those suffering

186

From depression and anxiety,
And possession by evil spirits.

Indeed, Jesus' powers of healing
Drew so much attention
That jealous religious leaders of that time
Hated Him for His gifts.

The Power Is Passed On

Jesus wished His powers for healing
To be passed on to His disciples:

"And as you go, proclaim
That the kingdom of heaven is close at hand.
Cure the sick, raise the dead,
Cleanse the lepers, cast out devils." Mt. 10:8

Jesus asked His disciples to have great faith.
Once when He was hungry
He found a fig tree, but it was barren.
He cursed the tree and it withered.
Then He told His disciples:

"I tell you solemnly,
If you have faith and do not doubt at all,
Not only will you do what I have done
To the fig tree, but even if you say to this mountain
'Get up and throw yourself into the sea,'
It will be done.
And if you have faith,
Everything you ask for in prayer
You will receive." Mt. 21:21-22

Jesus' miracles of healing
Were the signs of the coming
Of a new Power into our world,
The Holy Spirit.

"I tell you most solemnly,
Whoever believes in me

Will perform the same works as I do myself,
He will perform even greater works,
Because I am going to the Father . . .
I shall ask the Father,
And He will give you another Helper
To be with you forever,
That Spirit of truth
Whom the world can never receive
Since it neither sees nor knows Him;
But you know Him,
Because He is with you, He is in you." Jn. 14:12, 16-17

In the Early Church

After Jesus' death and resurrection,
The Apostles of the early Church
Carried on His work of healing:

"He was a cripple from birth;
And they used to put him down
Every day near the Temple entrance . . .
When this man saw Peter and John
On their way into the Temple
He begged from them...but Peter said,
'I have neither silver nor gold,
But I will give you what I have:
In the name of Jesus Christ the Nazarene, walk!'
Peter then took him by the hand
And helped him to stand up. Instantly
His feet and ankles became firm,
He jumped up, stood, and began to walk,
And he went with them into the Temple,
Walking and jumping and praising God." Acts 3:2-9

The leaders of the early Church also
Prayed over and anointed the sick
As James, a leader of the Jewish-Christian
Community in Jerusalem, commends:

188

"If one of you is ill,
He should send for the elders of the Church,
And they must anoint him with oil
In the name of the Lord
And pray over him. The prayer of faith
Will save the sick man and the Lord
Will raise him up again; and if he has
Committed any sins, he will be forgiven." James 5:14-15

Down Through the Ages

Down through the ages
The faithful in the Church
Have carried on this work of praying over
And anointing the sick.
Its full shape as a Sacrament
Took form in the Church
As the Anointing of the Sick.

The purpose of this prayer and anointing
Is to forgive our sins
And to help us overcome our sickness.
And if our time to die has come,
The prayers and anointing are to help
Bring us strength and a peaceful heart
For our journey with Christ
Into the next Life.

*   *   *   *   *   *

There is much more that could be written
About Christ's gift of His Spirit to us
For our health and life through
This Sacrament of prayer and anointing.
But let us end here for now.

7. A Note on the History of the Sacrament of the Anointing of The Sick in the Church.

From the beginning of the Church until about the ninth century the Anointing of the Sick was mainly for restoring health. The spiritual effects of the sacrament were not the main focus of attention. The prayer and anointing were for any sickness except very minor ones. Lay people, more commonly than priests, did the anointing.

After several centuries of change throughout the Christian Church, we find that from the twelfth century onward, only priests did the Anointing. The meaning of the sacrament became centered around the moment of dying; small children and some emotionally ill could not be anointed. The focus of attention became the spiritual life of the sick person and not the restoration of his physical well-being.

Today there is a return to the attitudes and practices of the early Church. What we had been accustomed to call "Extreme Unction" or "The Last Rites," has become again "The Anointing of the Sick." The focus is once again on healing. It is a prayer of faith to Jesus, asking Him to restore the whole person: body, soul, spirit, to health through the power of the Holy Spirit given through the Church. It is a prayer for the sick person's return to active life within the community. If it becomes clear that the time for a person to leave this life has come, then the prayer and the anointing are for the dying person's peace of heart, and strength of faith and love for the sometimes painful passage from death to eternal Life.

chapter eight

MARRIAGE AND FAMILY LIFE

"Have you come here freely . . .to give yourselves
To each other in married life?"

"Will you accept children lovingly from God
And bring them up according to the law of Christ
And His Church?"

From the Rite of Marriage

1. The Story of Indian Marriage And Family Life

INDIAN MARRIAGE

Marriage, Something To Be Respected

A good, lasting marriage has been always considered
Something wonderful, something to be respected,
Something good.
It brought comfort and happiness
To the husband and wife,
Life and stability to the whole band or tribe.

A typical marriage was arranged by the parents
Of the man and the woman. There was
An exchange of gifts between the families,
Signs of respect and good will. The bride's father
Received something honorable
For the gift of his daughter.

A man could have more than one wife
If his wealth permitted it,
Or if his position of leadership within the band
Required it. The Chief or Headman often
Offered hospitality to many visitors and guests:

*"He needed the assistance of a second or third wife
In order to prepare food
And gifts for the visitors."* Frank Halfmoon

Preparation for Marriage

There was strict order and discipline in the Indian family
That was for the good of everyone.
Young girls were protected;
They were kept separate from the boys

And busy working with their mothers and grandmothers
Until they became ready for marriage.

Boys were taught by their fathers and uncles
Self-discipline and self-sacrifice,
Courage and self-control in the face of
Fear and pain.

Discipline was very strict.
Even today among the grandparents
There are memories of whippings.
Girls and women were struck for immodest eyes,
Boys and men whipped for letting their desires go ahead
Of the good order of the bands.

Girls were raised to help their women Elders
With all of the camp work, keeping the fires,
Preparing the meat for drying or cooking,
Cleaning and storing the roots and berries.
The grandmothers considered it not good
For a young woman to be idle.

She was carefully taught to be a good wife
And mother, as she became more and more aware
Of her relationship to life and to the earth,
And to the awesome mystery of her gift
For bringing new life into the world.

Boys, raised hunting and fishing together
With their male Elders, learned to be
Father-providers for a family.

Both young men and women knew the old stories,
The Wisdom of their ancestors passed on to them
Through the joy of speaking, acting, singing.
Both knew the seeking of strength and vision
In the Sweathouse
And through solitude up in the high places.

The Coming of the Catholic Way

When the Blackrobes came,
They were welcome guests of the Chiefs.
But they asked that each man
Have only one wife. This was a difficult
Decision for some Chiefs and Headmen,
For often many came to their lodge for a smoke,
For a meal, for considering a choice for their People.

The Blackrobes also taught that
To participate in the Church,
To receive the Sacramental Life of the Church,
A couple had to be married in the Catholic Way.
The People saw this as a good Way,
A couple staying together on this earth
And walking into heaven together to join their Ancestors.

But for many, their first marriage did not work out.
This led to great sadness, for most valued highly
Being fully part of the Indian community
That now centered around the Mission Church.
This sadness, this sense of being separated,
Has lasted and lasted.

"Shacking Up"

There is a way of being together
We call "shacking up."
The Great-grandparents say they do not remember
This way being used till well into our present century.
The Elders do not feel this is the best way
For two to live together
And raise a family.
It is as if something holy, complete, and good
Is missing.

"It does not have the right permanence
For a clean and strong bond
Between parent and child." Frank Halfmoon

196

INDIAN FAMILY LIFE

The Gift of Life

Strong and ordered family life
Was always a most precious gift.
There was a right way,
A traditional way for doing everything.

For children, grandparents were a joy to be with.
They were truly wise and good and kind.
They knew the wonderful stories,
The correct ways of speaking, dancing, singing.

Grandparents were the living link with the Holy,
With those who had gone before.
They were a transparent reflection
Of the Holiness within each person
And within all things.

Children were a precious gift—
Life was harsh, sometimes cruel.
A child born safely was an occasion
Of immense joy.

A child growing and healthy was something wonderful,
Never taken for granted.
The child was someone treasured,
Yet given the freedom to learn, to adventure,
To risk, to choose.

One Family

The child belonged to all the People.
All those older were his Elders
And could teach and correct the child.

There was a sense of large family, which meant
Many brothers and sisters.
There was no word for "cousin."

It was very good to be with family,
Something terrible to be thrown out
Or torn away from family and band.

It was good to live on the same earth,
The same magical and storied places
That the Ancestors shared and enjoyed.
The People knew that they
Had been here forever.

The Separation

With the continual arrival of more non-Indians,
Everything changed at a bewildering speed.
The old people tried to keep family ways intact,
But it was difficult.

Children were sent off to far-away schools;
They were separated from their grandparents.
They were taught new ways of thinking and acting;
They learned to speak a different language.

Many grandparents encouraged their children
To go away to school, to learn
The white man's knowledge and language
Because they knew the world they loved
Was being shattered.

But the ways of the non-Indian were so different.
Indian grandparents didn't want their
Children to be humiliated,
Persecuted, treated as dust by the side of the road.
They wanted their children to survive,
To be proud. It was
A difficult choice.

The Bath of Pain

There were also terrible sicknesses
That came with the non-Indian:
Sicknesses that wiped out families
And cut whole bands in half.
The People knew no medicine against them.

Whiskey, white man's worst gift to the Indian,
Tore families once strong and stable
Into pieces. Some homes
Turned into violent nightmares.
The Mission school became a home
For children with nowhere else to go.

Husband and wife turned against each other,
Brother against brother, sister against sister.
Old people were abandoned and forgotten,
Forced to view helplessly the violent deaths
Of all their children, all their hopes.

The Tearing Away

Families were forced off the good land they loved,
The land their Ancestors had enjoyed forever.
Others wanted this land for farming,
While miners combed and gouged the hills for gold.

Bands and families that once enjoyed
Plenty of land for hunting and gathering,
Plenty of space for getting along with each other,
Were now told to gather into one tight place.

Because the whole way of living with the land
Was changed, life became even more
A battle for survival.
Family against family, band against band
Competed for favors from the conquering government,
Learning the way of twisting truth for self-advantage.

A wise, self-reliant, proud people became
"Wards" of the Government, prisoners of war,
A war that seemed to have no end.

Parents watched their houses bulldozed over,
Their Churches dragged to higher ground
As the waters rose behind a gigantic dam
And flooded the graves of their ancestors.
They were given little or no help in relocation.

"Even though they were 'told' this was going to happen
They could not believe it
Or even imagine it happening." Dr. Jay Miller

Did it help to give a few dollars
And empty promises to a sad-eyed chief?
Did it help to make big speeches
Before a broken-hearted People
Whose whole way of life had been drowned?

No salmon could jump over the Dams
To reach the rivers.
No salmon could make his way home
To feed the People at the Falls.
The Falls where Tribes had gathered
For six thousand years
Now slept under fifty feet of water.

The Uncertain Now

On the Reservation now there are few
Of the big trees that graced
And sheltered the land for centuries.
The hills once densely green
And full of life are now scarred
And laced with a network of roads
Going nowhere.

And now the challenge of the mine.
How will this powerful new industry
Affect family life? Will it help
Keep families and a People together
When the mountain is taken down?

All of the wars the men ever fought in
Hurt them even though they fought with courage.
They brought the war home within themselves,
All of the memories too terrible to forget.

Today stereos, TVs, movies,
Magazines blare values
That Great-great-grandparents would not recognize.
Young people are subjected
To all the fanciful flights and fads
Of the dominant society.
Drugs numb and drain away capacities
For a genuine experience
Of personal dignity, integrity, and power.

And Yet the Family Continues

In spite of all this pain and interruption,
Family life is still the most valued gift
On the Reservation or anywhere.
A man, a woman, a child without family
Is the saddest of persons.
There is a saying
That an Indian does not leave home
Until after he is fifty.
There is still truth in this saying.

Grandparents, parents, and children—
Despite tragedies and setbacks
That would have paralyzed a people less strong—
Still give themselves,
Still make the tremendous sacrifices,
Still live with the unextinguishable faith and love
That alone makes family life possible.

201

2. Marriage and Family in the Scriptures

The Sacrament of Marriage came out
Of the Church's growing understanding of herself.

God's Love for His Family

The Jewish people from olden times
Knew that strong marriage and family ties
Meant the very survival of their people:
They had strong laws protecting marriage.

They also experienced their Creator's
Care for them through history
As the Presence of His undying love
For them, His children.

"When Israel was a child I loved him,
And I called my son out of Egypt.
But the more I called to them,
The further they went from me;
They have offered sacrifice to the Baals
And set their offerings smoking before the idols.
I myself taught Ephraim to walk,
I took them in my arms;
Yet they have not understood
That I was the one looking after them.
I led them with reins of kindness,
With leading strings of love.
I was like someone who lifts an infant
Close to his cheek;
Stooping down to him I gave him his food." Hosea 11:1-4

Jesus' Love for His Body, the Church

The Christian communities that grew and unified
After Christ's death and Resurrection
Also knew that strong marriage and family life

Were essential for preserving the fabric of
Their new society.

They, too, increasingly reflected on marriage not only
As the image of the Creator's love for His People,
But also as the image of the union of Christ
With His Body, the Church.

"For this reason, a man must leave
His father and mother
And be joined to his wife,
And the two will become one body.
This mystery has many implications; but I am saying
It applies to Christ and the Church.
To sum up; you too, each one of you, must love his wife
As he loves himself; and let every wife
Respect her husband." Ephesians 5:31-33

Jesus' Love of Family

Jesus Himself, at the request of His mother,
Performed His first miracle at a wedding in Cana
So that His hosts would not be embarassed,
And the wedding celebration could continue.

He had great respect for marriage and family life.
His own mother and father were good parents
Who looked after Him and cared for Him
Though they were very poor.

He spent thirty years at home
Working with His dad,
Obedient to His parents.

"He went down with them and came to Nazareth
And lived under their authority. His mother
Stored up all these things in her heart.
And Jesus increased in wisdom, in stature, and in favor
With God and man." Luke 2:15-52

After Joseph's death
Mary continued to look after Jesus
During His public life of traveling and teaching.

Jesus' New Family: Us

When He was dying on the cross,
He gave His mother to His Beloved Disciple
To take care of. And so Mary
Became the mother of the Apostles,
The mother of the Church.

"Seeing his mother and the disciple he loved
Standing near her, Jesus said to his mother,
'Woman, this is your son.' Then to the disciple he said,
'This is your mother.' And from that moment
The disciple made a place for her
In his home." John 19:26-27

And so it is not hard to see
How the Church came to treasure
The marriages of her People,
Marriages that grew into family lives,
As images of Jesus' own family
And of His own love and care for us.

The Church grew to consider marriage vows
As holy, sacred, and blessed.
Marriage became one of the Sacraments of the Church,
One of the special ways Christ's Presence,
His Love and Peace, is invited more and more
Into our broken world.

Marriage as the Image of Our Future

It is not an accident
That in Revelations (the book that completes
The New Testament) the writer,
Hurt and angry over the terrible persecution

204

Of his Christian brothers and sisters,
Cries out with the Church to Jesus,
Risen in victory over pain and death,
To please hurry in His coming to help.

In his vision of the end of time
He sees the Church as a Bride
Suffering, yet filled with immense Spirit,
Her eyes fixed firmly on her Beloved.

*"The Spirit and the Bride say, 'Come.' . . .
Amen; come, Lord Jesus."* Rev. 22:17-20

3. Christian Marriage and Love

LOVE, LOVE, DESIRE

> *"For love is strong as Death . . .
> The flesh of it is a flash of fire,
> A flame of Yahweh (God) himself."*
> Song of Songs 8:6-7

There is Love

LOVE,
This is our Creator,
Father, Son, Spirit.

Love, Full, Complete,
Spilling out into all creation,
Holding, nourishing
All that is real, all that lasts forever.

This is the perfect Love,
Wishing to fully communicate Itself,
That suddenly, without warning,
Breaks in upon us
And floods our hearts to their breaking points
With assurance of Concern and Peace
Beyond our understanding.

It is this Love which,
When we are given awareness of it,
Makes us weep—
We are so hurt, so overwhelmed,
So taken beyond where we thought we were headed.
It is this Love
Which changes us, makes it possible
For us to love.

Our Love

There is love.
This is our love,
The best our hearts and minds can offer.
This love is the mirror of Love
And the gift of Love.

Fire igniting fire,
Flame sustaining flame,
The one within the Other,
Becoming One.

This love held within Love
A little flower (poor, fragile, delicate)
Offered as a gift
Within the Gift.

Precious is this love,
Something beyond our needs,
Our ups and downs; this love,
A choice remembered
And each day renewed
With the hope of lasting forever.

Desire

There is desire.
We also have the joy and distinction
Of being bodies,

Bodies made for seeing, touching,
And embracing.
Desire, too, is the gift, the
Mirror of Perfect Love,
Reaching out, growing, expanding.

It is a yearning,
A burning for union
From deep within the human heart
And from within the Heart of Love Itself.

Fire within Fire,
Fire begetting joy and more love,
Fire begetting children of love.

All these are very good.
These three are our natural heritage and inheritance:
To be full of Love, love, and desire.

To be like our Father
Full of Love for the world,
To be like Jesus
Full of love and truth,
To be full of the Spirit,
Groaning till all creation is set free—
Nothing else
Really expresses our greatness.

This is something towards the fullness
Of the mystery we hope to honor
And express through the Sacrament of Marriage.

MARRIAGE AND LOVE

Two Becoming One

A man and a woman,
Each wishing the happiness of the other,
Choose to make life together,

The two becoming one
Becoming many.

Two friends
Open to the gift of Love,
Their love.
It is wonderful and mysterious
How two distinct
And individual hearts and minds
Can hope to grow into
A union of hearts and minds.

It is best if this is done
In some freedom; our needs,
Our expectations are so many.
They began when we were children.

Our Tremendous Needs:

The need to be close, intimate,
The need to be separate, away alone;
The need to be lost in the beauty
Of the life of the other,
The need to be lost in the joy
Of our own life, our own self.

Most of us do not
Come to marriage very free.
We wish to share, to give,
But we also want
A lot for ourselves.

We have so many needs from childhood:
To be wanted, to be held,
To be warmed and consoled,
To be understood.

We have so many scars from adolescence
That so badly need healing. We need
To be comforted and reassured

That we are all right being who we are
So we can dare to reach out
And to trust again.

This struggle within us is normal and good,
For from this battle inside us
Over what we think we can give
And what we think we can't
Comes our growth and self-knowledge.

Walking With Our Fear

Walking together up the mountain
Sometimes one of us, sometimes both
Of us stumble and fall.
Sometimes one has to go back
And pick the other up.
But there is always the desire
To walk together.

Most of us are faithful and unfaithful.
Love is what we want the most
And what we avoid the most.
We lose our Way
Which is to sacrifice, to give away ourselves.

Instead we try to take something for ourselves.
We are so afraid
That if we give away everything,
There will be nothing left
For us to be us,
That we will simply disappear!

Evil always uses this fear
To keep us from loving,
To convince us of the greatest lie there is:
That we are not capable of being loved,
That we are not capable of loving.

The Pain of Growing in Love

Loving is always painful.
If we love and are loved,
We are going to be hurt;
We are going to hurt the one we love.

We are going to be understood
And not understood.
We are going to understand
And not understand.
We will try to explain, to convince,
And we will fail.

We are going to yearn to be together
And wish to be apart. Our hearts
Are going to feel soft and compassionate,
Hard and cruel,
Peaceful and calm,
Tired and restless.
All these things are part of us.

We are going to wish to be simple,
To reveal everything about ourselves;
We will want to hold in and hide.
There are feelings in us so complex and dark,
We do not dare to share them.

But if we do not enter this bath of pain,
Risking to reach out, to give ourselves to others,
If we do not go forward,
Vulnerable and covered with wounds
That all can see,
Then we come to know a greater pain,
The hell of being truly alone.

"I tell you, most solemnly,
Unless a wheat grain falls on the ground and dies,
It remains only a single grain;
But if it dies,
It yields a rich harvest." Jn. 12:24

LOVE IS THE PRESENCE OF OUR CREATOR IN THE WORLD

"I will love them with all my heart,
For all my anger has turned from them."

Hos.14:5

"Husbands should love their wives just
As Christ loved the Church and sacrificed
Himself for her to make her holy."

Eph. 5:25

The Love of the Father

Our Father-Creator
Is always seen in the Old Testament
As One who loves us, His sons and daughters,
His people.

He loves our world. He is
A jealous Lover who wishes our love
In return. He wants us to love only
What is true and lasting and good.

Too often we are unfaithful, fickle,
Wandering, our hearts made of stone.
Too often we are a curse rather than a blessing
To His children: the poor, the oppressed,
The broken, the forgotten.
Too often we forget Him,
The very One who made us.

The Love of Jesus

In the New Testament
Jesus comes among us,
The fulfillment of God's promise
Of love and forgiveness.

211

Because of Jesus alive in and with us
We can dare to love, to begin again,
No matter how many times we have fallen.
We can dare to dream of a whole world
Where all are brothers and sisters.

He is our Elder Brother.
We are His family, His People.
He is so full of love for us,
So full of joy in our presence,
That the writers tell us
He is like a Bridegroom, completely faithful,
Bursting with joy over us
His Bride, the Church.

The Couple as the Mirror of the Love Of Jesus and the Father

The bridegroom is to love his bride
As totally and unselfishly as Jesus
Loves all of us, His Church.
The bride is to give herself
To help her husband, the way
We desire to give ourselves to Christ.

Heaven is seen as the greatest Wedding Feast
We will ever attend.
And everyone we ever reached out to
(The little ones, the forgotten, the despised)
Will be there to share it with us.

The Couple's Journey Is the Assurance That There Is Love in the World

For a married couple
Their journey toward God
Is a journey together.

A husband loves and trusts his wife.
He is willing to give his life
For the safety and health of his family.

A wife loves and cares for her husband.
She gives her whole life for his well-being,
And for the health and protection of their children.

By their life of faithfulness to each other
And devotion to their children,
And their life of sacrifices
For the good of the whole community,
Married couples are meant to assure us all
That there is love in our world—
Kind, merciful, creative love.

Marriage: The Experience of Jesus and the Spirit

Within the Church
Marriage has become a Sacrament:
A unique and powerful experience of Jesus
Present and active within us.

The joy we feel at a marriage
Is from the breath of His Spirit
Breathing Life, His Love, into us.

4. Preparing for Marriage And Family Life

It is good to meet with the Priest or Deacon
Six months to a year ahead of the day
Chosen for the marriage.
This gives ample time to prepare
For this special day.

There are many opportunities nowadays
For couples to strengthen their confidence in,
Their knowledge of, and appreciation for each other.
There are cassettes and writings, retreat weekends
And evenings that many find enriching, encouraging.

It is good to talk over with the Priest or Deacon
And with other mature couples, if possible,
Feelings about marriage,
Expectations of each other.

Here Are Some Possible Questions to Consider:

What attracts me to this person?
Why do I want to be with this person forever?

*What Strengths, What Weaknesses Do I Bring
To My Partner?*

What strengths, what weaknesses does my partner
Bring to me?
What fears or worries do I have? Are they real?
Am I ready to leave my parents' family
To begin my own family,
Respecting the one I love?

*What Does Being Married in the Church
Mean to Us?*

Does this add anything to our lives together?
What do we wish to say to each other
And be for each other?
How do the Catholic people in our community
Understand marriage?
What do we wish to say to them?
What do they look for in us? What is expected of us?
What support can we expect from the
Catholic community?

*What Things Will Strengthen, What Things
Will Weaken Our Marriage?*

Will we spend our evenings at home together?
On weekends will we enjoy our free times together?
Or will we choose separate paths?
Are major family decisions made by both of us?

How Many Children Do We Want? How Soon?

Will we both be helping at their birth, with their growing?
How will we share our Faith with them?

How Much Money Do We Need to Be Content?

What are our financial goals?
Do we plan on renting, or on owning our own house?
Are we both agreeable to family or friends
Sharing our home?
Are we both going to work?
How do we feel about both of us working
And caring for our home?
Are we in agreement about where we will live?
Will we do any moving away from home?

*Have We Ever Prayed Together? Do We Have
Ways of Praying? Do We Ever Go to Church Together?*

How do we feel about prayer and the Church?
What do we feel toward the people that are the Church in
This town? Is there some couple whose life
We look up to?

*How Have We Both Experienced the Presence
Of Our Creator in Our Lives?*

How do we understand Him?
Are we aware of Jesus Present to us?
Do we want to know Him better?

Are There Memories, Hurts, Fears
That Haunt and Depress Me,

That hold me back from trusting, loving?
Things I would like
To ask Jesus to free me of? (This question may be better
To consider just with the priest.)

Alcohol. What Part Does It Play in Our Life Together?

Does it hurt or build our love and trust in each other
And toward our Creator? What happens when one of us
Or both of us drink?
Does our drinking help or hinder our feeling of dignity,
Self-worth, spiritual strength?

Marijuana. What Part Does It Play in Our Life Together?

Do we need it all the time?
Do we need it at all?

Sacrifice. Do We See It as an Expression of Our Love?

Or is sacrifice something we expect others to do for us?
Are my own sacrifices ones that demand recognition
Or are they done freely in the spirit of helping my spouse?

Anger, Frustration: How Do I Act When I Get Mad?

What things do I do? Do I get rough with or beat
Up my spouse? Do I sulk or pout? Do I blame others for
My own problems?

What Was My Parents' Marriage Like?

How did they show their love for each other?
How did they show their anger? What things have I learned
From my parents' or grandparents' marriage?

Forgiving: Can We Forgive and Forget the Hurts

We have caused in each other? Are there things we can do
That will help us to do this?
What amends are we willing to make?

Do We Wish to Be More by Ourselves or More Involved

In our little town? Are there children or friends
Or elders that need our eyes and ears or hands?
Are there situations in our town that need changing?
Is there some little thing we could do to help?

There Are Many in Our World Who Are Oppressed:

They are starving, they are without homes, without work,
Without hope. Is there anything we could give away to
Show we care, that we are with them,
That we have not forgotten them?

The Entire World Of Nature,

The delicate and beautiful Earth that provides our food,
The water we drink, the air we breathe, the wood and oil
For warmth and travel, the animals we eat or watch
And delight in—all this is threatened by overdevelopment.
How do we feel about this? Is there anything we can
Sacrifice to make things better?
Can we be better informed
On the consequences of over-mining, over-logging, and
Over-grazing? Do we know how we can make our
Concerns heard by the Tribal Council,
Or by City, County, State and Federal Governments?

*War. Annihilation. Man Now Has the Power to
Poison the Earth*

So that nothing will grow, to poison the air
So that every living thing dies convulsing in agony,

To poison our bodies so that none survives the sickness.
Man has created weapons of war powerful enough to
Destroy the earth, to kill each of us ten times over.
What do we feel in the face of this presence of Evil?
Is there anything we can do to stop our building
Toward this holocaust? Do we feel that war happens only
In other countries?

Our Town, Our Country, Our World
Are Being Torn to Pieces by Violence.

Is there anything we can do to stop this?

CONFESSION BEFORE MARRIAGE

It is good, sometime during preparation for marriage,
To experience Jesus working powerfully
Through the Sacrament of Reconciliation.

Jesus, working through this Sacrament,
Can help us with our heavy burdens of sadness and guilt,
Our bogged-down heaviness of mind and heart.
He does this by taking most of the load on Himself.

Through the presence and the words of His priest,
Jesus can assure us of His unconditional love for us.
He can fill us with new clearness and light.
He can give us strong feelings of self-worth and goodness,
The ground of our ability to love.

Jesus can fill us with the gift of His Spirit,
Encouraging us to set out on our new journey
Fresh, full of hope.

5. Promising Love Forever

*"This is why a man leaves his father
And mother and joins himself to his
Wife, and they become one body."*
Gen. 2:24

In the Ceremony of Christian Marriage

We stand in truth before our Creator, our Father,
Before our family and friends,
Before our Ancestors who pray for us.

We say before our Creator and His People
This is the one I love,
This is the one I will cherish all my life.

This mystery we participate in,
We live in Him,
We welcome Him more into our lives,
We give Him thanks,
We suffer, yet we trust
That He will never leave us.

*We Ask Our Father to Forgive Us and to Help Us,
For We Easily Lose Our Way.*

We wish to begin new and fresh together
"Lord, have mercy on us."

We Listen to His Word to Us in Scripture,

His respect and concern for us,
His promise to be with us.

Priests and Elders may wish
To share their heart with us
Or offer a prayer or song to help us.
It is good if we can share our heart with them.

We Make Our Vows to Each Other,

A promise of love forever.
Rings are blessed and given,
The signs of hearts blessed, given,
And bound together.

Bread and Wine Are Offered,

Signs of life and love fully accepted
And given back in joy.
All creation is honored,
Especially the gift of Love to us:
Marriage and family.

Through Our Faith in Him

(Taking the bread and wine, doing
What He asked us to do in His memory)
Jesus becomes Present among us
In an intensely special way,
Offering His life for us to the Father,
Giving His life to us in love.

We Ask for the Gift of His Spirit

To be poured out upon His whole Church,
Upon us the living,
Upon all those who have gone ahead of us.

We Pray the "Our Father,"

The prayer our Lord taught us,
Asking humbly to be a true son,
A true daughter,
Generous and kind,
Faithful in love.

During Communion We Receive Jesus

Into our hearts together,
A sign of our union with Him
And our closeness to each other.
This Blessed Bread broken and shared among us
Is the strength for our journey together.

At the End of Mass

We bow our heads
Before Him and His People, asking for
Deep and lasting love,
His peace and harmony in our home,
Children to share our joy,
Loyal friends who will encourage us
To stay together,
Brothers and sisters who need our help,
And, most of all, the Creator
At the very Center of our hearts together—
Father, Son, and Spirit.

This Prayer is Not a Selfish Thing.

We fully expect that Jesus will change us,
Expand our love, till our hearts
Embrace the whole world,
Every man, woman and child,
All things alive and breathing,
Every creature given to us for our care.

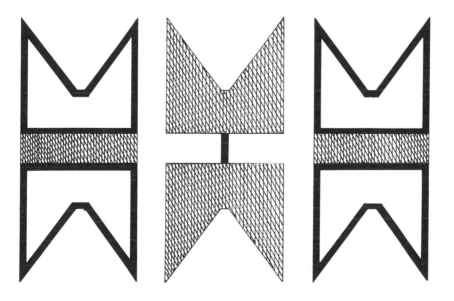

6. After Marriage, What?

The more we give ourselves away
The more we are, within.

Jesus was a man for others.

"His state was divine,
Yet he did not cling
To his equality with God
But emptied Himself
To assume the condition of a slave,
And became as men are;
And being as all men are,
He was humbler yet,
Even to accepting death,
Death on a cross.
But God raised him high
And gave him the name
Which is above all other names . . ."

Ph. 2:6-11

The Circles of Growth

There are many ups and downs,
The inevitable cycles of growth
(The circles of life to death to life that hold us)
The fights that erupt when two people
Really care about each other.

These shouldn't unduly surprise us,
Or cause us to lose heart,
But they usually do.

The Dying

Being together,
Talking with each other,
(Once easy and delightful)
Becomes difficult and repulsive.

222

Feelings once shared
Are pulled inwards.

Children, once a miracle,
A proud joy beyond speaking,
Become a jangling, noisy burden.
The job, once enjoyable
Because it was honest and good and stretched us,
Becomes intolerable. We can't go on.

Everything begins to look and feel wrong.
The closeness of those who know us
Suffocates us. We want to run from them.
We don't want to be home
And when we are home, we want to be alone.

We feel tired and restless.
Making love is impossible;
We want no one close to even touch us.

We take off with the gang,
Smoke and drink until we can't feel the pain
Building inside.
We start trouble, fight,
Jump into other beds.
It all goes nowhere.
We want to cry, to scream, to kill ourselves.

Nothing seems to help.
Nothing seems to matter.
Prayer is impossible.
Even the Creator isn't close. At best
He's a remote possibility,
A wild card that only the priest or our grandparents
Have hidden up their sleeve.

We feel cut off from everyone,
Especially those we hoped to spend our life with.
We feel hateful to ourselves
And to everyone. We no longer have any respect
For ourselves or others.
We are truly alone.

The Rising

If we are lucky we finally look for help.
Where is it?
It's always inside ourselves.
We begin to listen to ourselves.

What's wrong? It used to be so good!
We go out alone. We drive.
We talk to ourselves and to someone we trust.
Slowly we begin to dare to come into contact
With what we are feeling,
This mass of powerful and twisted feelings inside.

If we are lucky
We dare to be honest,
To really look at what we are thinking, feeling,
What we are doing to ourselves
And to the ones we love.

We dare to ask our Maker for help,
Because in the deep recesses of our memory
We recall there was mentioned One
Who would help when no others would.

We risk trusting Him, believing
In His power to change us,
To be our Friend
Even though we feel so unworthy
Of this or any friendship.

With His help we begin to see
And to admit our sins, our faults, our selfishness.
We see our failures in a new, constructive light.
They have brought us more truth about our needs
And more awareness of the Creator
Present and Loving us.

We desire to forgive
And to ask for forgiveness.
We want to start again, to give
And be given another chance.

If we have a partner who is willing
To suffer and die and rise with us,
Then we do begin again.
Everything becomes real again,
New and fresh and alive,
Especially our Creator and the ones we love.

If our children are old enough,
We ask their forgiveness and trust again.
If they are little
We hold them as if for the first time,
The noisy cartoon on TV seen through tears
And a long ways away.

All the pain was for giving birth
To a new person. All the dying
Was really so that there could be more life.
We are like the snake
That has to shed his skin
Because the old skin cannot contain
All the growth that is coming forth from within.

The Gift Love Gives

This terrible and wonderful struggle,
This dying and being given new life
Is the gift of Love to us
Freely given. We could not endure
Our struggle to be born again
Over and over unless someone noticed us,
Held us, looked at us, cared for us,
Showed us we mattered,
Gave us their time here on this earth.

225

This is the mystery of Jesus' regard for us,
This is the way He looks towards us
And feels about us and reaches out
To grasp our hand and to embrace us.
This alone is what saves us from a lonely death.

And this is our mystery,
That in our limited way, with our tiny hearts
We grant one another and every living thing
Death or life.
Love alone overcomes death.

There is really nothing else to be or do
More important than
To give our whole attention to someone,
Especially someone whom no one else notices.
While wishing nothing for ourselves, we want
To really see her, hear her, touch her
And in her to See Him, Hear Him, Touch Him.
Such a self-forgetful way of loving
Cannot be pretended.

It is something we are incapable of doing alone
Because of our fear of the dark side of ourselves
And our fear of one another.
We are enabled to love this way
Only through the gift of our Creator's Spirit
Poured into our hearts and, through them, to others.
We are enabled to love this way
Through the strength given us
By those who have truly loved us.

In the last analysis,
Everything we really are and
Everything we really give of importance,
Is already first given to us
By those who loved us.

"I have been crucified with Christ, and the life
I live now is not my own; Christ is living in me.
I still live my human life, but it is a life
Of faith in the Son of God, who loved me
And gave himself for me." Gal. 2:19b-20

Taking the Time

It is good to take the time
Just to be man and woman together.
It is good to go out together again for
A movie, a dinner, a weekend
Away from all our other cares.
It is good to take the time
To discover each other again.

It is good to gather as couples
To relax, to be happy, to talk,
To pray and offer Mass together.

We gather, knowing ever more deeply
The sacrifices we have all been called to make,
The terrible struggle we have all
Been asked to endure

So that we all become
More free and shining,
More full of the joy and peace He has promised us,
If we walk this journey with Him together.

* * * * * *

There is much more that could be written
About the joy, the struggle, the peace
That the sacrament of marriage
Brings into our lives,
But let us end here for now.

7. Some Things to Consider

Family Planning

The Church considers human life sacred,
Precious, of inestimable value
From the moment of its beginning.
The holiness of the child is linked inseparably
To the Holiness of the Creator.

This gift of a person is from the depths
Of the Person Jesus Himself.
The Life sustaining the breath of the child
Is the very Spirit of our Creator.

The Church in North America encourages us
To be intelligent, generous, and responsible
In considering the size of our family.
This is not easy,
For a delicate balance is required
Of self-sacrifice and good sense.

There are many factors to be considered.
Reflecting on our way of helping
Within our community and world,
How many children can we care for,
(Either our own or others)
In a strong, healthy, supportive way
All the years they need us?

How is our mental, physical, spiritual
Sense of strength and well-being holding up?
Will many children be a joy
Or too great a burden for us?
Do we weigh down the children we already have
With worries and responsibilities too heavy for them?

Birth and Bonding

One of the bright aspects of contemporary family life
Is the role husbands are encouraged to play
In helping their wives prepare for birth.

From the earliest stages of pregnancy
The husband is encouraged to understand
And support his wife as she cares
For the life growing within her.

He is sensitive to her need for rest,
To her changes in mood, reassuring her
When she begins to doubt her beauty, her strength,
Her self-worth as a wife and mother.

Couples learn and practice together
Natural methods of childbirth.
Dad is in the delivery room as well as Mom
And he is one of the first to hold close to his heart
The new arrival. This bonding between
Both parents and child
Is the perfect beginning
For a bond of love that lasts forever.

Married Couples and Their Priests

Married couples and their priests
Have a very close relationship.
The couples' example encourages him
To continue to give himself, to make sacrifices,
To remain faithful in his love
For all the People.

Priests, in turn, help couples by
Bringing them the strength of the Sacraments,
Being a good ear, a supportive friend,
Encouraging them not
To give up on each other.

A good and faithful priest
Is a witness of Faith, self-sacrifice,
Love, and hope to a married couple.
A strong and happy couple
Is the most encouraging sign for a priest
That the Creator's love is active in the world.
He, too, needs the joy of family
And the warmth of home very much.

Marriage Counseling

For couples who feel communication between them
Has seriously broken down,
There is available sound marriage counseling
By men and women trained for this work.

Sessions with a good counselor can be an occasion
For the beginning of a healing of relationships,
A bringing to light of feelings and memories
That have wounded hearts and crippled
The ability to trust and to give oneself.

There can be growth in self-knowledge
And respect for our partner, and new abilities
To talk to each other about feelings which before
We were unable to bring out.

Tribal and County counseling services usually
Provide such trained help.
So does Catholic Family Services
Sponsored by the Diocese.

Elders, too, are usually willing to listen
With hearts full of kindness and wisdom.
It is good to go see them
And sit and talk with them.

Alcohol and Drug Addiction

Couples suffering the sicknesses

Of alcoholism or drug addiction,
Should know that there is hope,
Even if one or both partners
Have hit the bottom.

Out of the darkness, the cold despair,
A tiny flame of hope still burns,
The desire to love and be loved again,
The desire to be responsible, serene,
Whole and well again.

In the midst of this darkness
Of the total exhaustion of our limited human power
To pull ourselves upward,
We can be born again from within
To become a new person in living, personal
Touch and friendship with the Source
Of all personal strength and goodness.

Sometimes a man or woman can go this route
Alone, confident that they are indeed a new person,
Relying on the Presence of unlimited Strength
Within them.

Sometimes, humbly leaving ourselves open
To the counseling given in treatment centers
Is invaluable in bringing us to a new and more complete
Awareness of ourselves.

The terribly demanding honesty of the AA
And Al-Anon programs has been an immense support for
And source of growth to many men and women
Who are strong leaders
In our Reservation communities today.

What is of most importance
Is that we dare to be open and honest
About our strengths and weaknesses
And the first to offer our hand
To any man or woman struggling to be free
Of this sickness that has always been
Our death as individuals and as a People.

Couples' Retreats and Marriage Encounter

The strength in these weekends is Jesus
Present, free, and shining through
The couples who lead these retreats.

We enter into a great mystery here:
The mystery of our Lord suffering, broken,
Vulnerable, dying, yet giving great life—
Our Lord, hidden Light in the lives
Of all those who suffer with Him
Pain that gives birth to a new awareness,
A new way of living.

The couples who give these retreats
Make us suddenly more aware of
The beauty, the growth, the endurance of their marriages,
Marriages that are wracked (like ours)
With doubt, selfishness, sickness,
Fighting, unfaithfulness, worry,
Fear, non-communication, alcoholism,
Yet show the miracle of life,
Life that grows and multiplies itself.

Because these couples love us,
The least of their brothers and sisters,
We become more alive, more free, more daring.
The good we see in them, we discover in ourselves.

Their openness becomes our openness.
Their honesty becomes our honesty.
Their courage in the face of pain becomes our courage.
Their prayer becomes our prayer.
Their Faith strengthens our Faith.
Their desire to give themselves away for others
Becomes our desire to give our life away for others.

Homosexuality

The Church has never felt that the sexual union
Of two men or of two women,
Or the marriage of men to men,
Or the marriage of women to women,
Is fully good for a man or a woman.

However, having someone who knows us,
Who cares about us, who wishes to be with us
And encourages us to live
Is certainly a greater good than being
Forsaken, despised, abandoned, alone.

The homosexual man or woman is to be loved,
Respected, cared for the same as anyone else.
The hope is that this bond of loving acceptance
Will engender trust, growth, openness,
Strength, the felt Presence of Jesus
Loving unconditionally, reaching out to help.

The hope is that this genuine concern
Will be the ground for a richer,
More powerful and more satisfying spiritual, emotional,
And social life for our brother or sister
Who so much needs our friendship.

Divorced Christians

The life-giving, faithful love of husband and wife
That goes through this life into the next
Is still the ideal of the Church.
It is a creative life
Of continual sacrifice. It involves
A growing mutual trust and respect,
Continual efforts to speak, to listen,
To learn, to forgive, to pray,
To begin again and again.
It is an ideal that requires the support

And the active and continuous encouragement
Of the whole community.

Not everyone is able to find
Or to live this ideal. Married life sometimes
Just does not work out between a man and a woman.
Things sometimes get so bad
That there is no longer a possibility of life together.

This brings great anger, confusion,
Guilt, sadness into a home.
Children become very unsure of themselves,
Anxious about the worth of their lives.
There is much need for reconciliation,
For rebuilding close ties,
The trust that holds a family together.

In times well within our memory,
Couples who lost their marriage
Were told they were excommunicated,
Cast out from the Christian community,
No longer able to receive the Sacraments
Of the Roman Catholic Church.

This was a severe punishment
And carried with it a heavy sadness,
A feeling of being thrown out
From the Catholic community with no possibility
Of being forgiven and allowed to return.

Today the Church, always imperfect,
Always learning, always wanting to be
More in the image of Christ,
Wants divorced Catholics to still feel and be an active
Part of the Christian community.

Divorced Catholics, sinful, yet forgiven,
Now have reason to be
Full of hope in Christ's kind Love,
Present in a special way in the Sacraments of the Church.
For it is His Love that changes us and makes us
New people, ready to begin again.

The Annulment of a Marriage Within the Church

The Church reaches out with Love
To her divorced couples.

The Formal Annulment

For very serious reasons,
There is the possibility of the annulment
Of a marriage that has taken place within the Church.
A formal process is conducted by the priest,
At the request of one of the divorced partners.

The priest interviews the person requesting
The annulment and, possibly, some witnesses
From the community whom the person might suggest.

The priest then submits this information
To the Bishop's representative
For consideration and judgment.

If the annulment is granted,
Both parties receive formal notice
Of this judgment in writing.
They are then free to remarry in the Church,
If they wish.

The priest usually concentrates his attention
On factors within the personal lives of the couple
Or on forces and influences from the larger community
That kept the marriage from ever becoming
What it was meant to be,
The mirror of the Creator's love for us in Jesus Christ.

The "Good Faith" Solution

Sometimes the priest knows divorced people
Who have remained loyal and faithful
In their devotion to Jesus and to His People, the Church.
Yet he knows that a formal annulment procedure
Would prove too difficult or be impossible to accomplish.

235

He may then in private assure them that
They are still welcome within the Church
And encourage them to re-enter joyfully
The Life given through the Sacraments of the Church.

8. An Historical Note on the Church And Marriage

Many of the customs we associate with marriage today, date back to the pre-Christian Mediterranean and European worlds. The bridal cake, the marriage veil, the exchange of rings, carrying the bride over the threshold of her new home: these were all customs in pre-Christian cultures.

In the Hebrew culture human sexuality was considered sacred. Early Hebraic law allowed a man more than one wife. Divorce was permitted, but as time went on the lifelong faithfulness of a man and woman in marriage became the praised ideal.

Jesus, in three of the Gospel stories spoke against divorce. St. Paul praised the union of husband and wife as the expression of Christ's love for His body, the Church. He also allowed for separation if one of the partners was an unbeliever and wished to separate from the believing partner. I Cor. 7:12-16

In the early Church marriages were contracted under civil law. By the Fourth century there is evidence of a priestly blessing for the couple's new life together.

In the fifth century there were liturgical celebrations of marriages. The father's consent, or the mutual consent of the couple was considered the essential part of the marriage.

There was a breakdown of social order in the West from the eighth century onward, and the Church became more involved in the legal aspects of marriage.

In the sixteenth century the Council of Trent required that the Christian marriage contract be public and that a priest be present. A trend began toward more freedom of choice in

236

regard to marriage partners, and by the seventeenth century, freedom from parental force was safeguarded. The sincere mutual consent of the marriage partners made the sacrament a reality.

Until relatively recently the Catholic marriage rite was in Latin, except for the vows, which were always in the language of the people. After 1960 the whole ceremony was in the language of the people.

Before 1935, marriage vows between Roman Catholics and members of other Christian Churches could not be received inside the Church building proper. Today the Church encourages partners in a "mixed" marriage to exchange their vows in the sanctuary and, if they wish, during a Nuptial Mass.

The Roman Catholic Church always fully recognizes the Sacrament of Marriage as celebrated in the other Christian Churches and will allow her own members the freedom to marry before a minister of another Christian Church, if there are good reasons for doing this.

Since the Second Vatican Council (1965) the Church has encouraged couples to be well informed and creative in planning their wedding so that it most fully expresses the unique history of the love and hope given them to share with their People.

9. Prayers

Marriage Vows Most Commonly Used

I Take You to Be My Wife. I Promise to Be True to You in Good Times and in Bad, in Sickness and in Health. I Will Love You and Honor You All the Days of My Life.

I Take You to Be My Husband. I Promise to Be True to You in Good Times and in Bad, in Sickness and in Health. I Will Love You and Honor You All the Days of My Life. From the Rite of Marriage

chapter nine

WAYS OF HELPING
THE PEOPLE HOME

"I am the good shepherd:
The good shepherd is one
Who lays down his life for his sheep."

Jn. 10:10

1. Indian Ways of Leadership

"I shall put my spirit in you
And you will live . . . ."
Ez. 37:14a

For thousands of years
The Creator provided
Strong and gifted men and women
Who could lead and help their People.
The bands could not survive without wise,
Strong, moral and spiritual leaders.

There were ceremonial chiefs
Who led the prayer of the People.
There were hunting chiefs
And a salmon chief.
The main chief, the son of chiefs,
Or a man chosen by his people to lead,
Directed the overall movement of the band.

It was his way
To consult the Elders
And the other chiefs, listening carefully
Before making a decision on matters
Concerning the welfare of his People.

He was expected to be
A man of courage, integrity, and wisdom.
His decisions could mean
The life or death of his People.

There were medicine men,
Bluejays, who could appear and disappear,
Going many miles in an instant,
Seeing and finding what
No one else could see or find.
These men sometimes had powers
For healing even the very sick.

There were gifts of power
For warriors, hunters, and fishermen.
There were men and women with powers
For winning at gambling.
The people enjoyed the stick game
And liked racing fast horses.

Grandmothers, mothers, and wives,
Held together the families
That made up the band.

They worked hard
Preparing the meat, the salmon,
The roots and berries, the shelter,
The clothing and fire which warmed the hearts
Of their husbands and children.

They knew well the secrets
For bringing beauty
And new life into the world.

They knew the healing roots, plants, and herbs.
They knew the making of richly designed
Bags and cedar baskets.

They were women of great Presence,
Wise and spiritual. Often they could heal
Wounded hearts and ailing bodies.

To be near a great woman of the band
Was to be near royalty.
Nearness to her brought a feeling of peace
As if one were really home.

2. The Circle of Powers Broken And Restored

I am indebted to Johnny Arlee
For the way of telling this story
In terms of a Circle of Powers.
He expressed this mystery
Of Spiritual Gifts shared among many
In a unique and creative manner
Which I can only poorly imitate here.

The First Circle

In the days of the original Indians
There was a strong sense of the mysterious,
The Sacred, present in all things,
The earth, the sky, the sun and moon.

The trees, rocks, the streams and wind,
The clouds and lightning,
In these a man or woman could encounter
The Holy, something with Power.

Powers given for helping, leading, healing,
Could be seen as a whole circle of powers
In which all people could share,
Be part of, if it came to them.

It took many gifts of power
To many individuals to make up
The Circle of Powers that was
The sustaining force of a band, a People.

242

These powers were all under the Creator,
"The one up above."
They came to individuals
When they were placed out alone as children
To see if they would be given a gift:
A helper, a song with power.

These things were experienced and respected.
The people knew how to live
And work with these powers.

The Circle Broken

When the non-Indians came
This whole world was interrupted.
There was great darkness and emptiness.

The white man could not see
Or appreciate the Indian world.
He did not usually respect it.
He had his own view of the earth,
His own powers and sources of power.
He had his own way of doing things.

The Blackrobes thought the Indians
Were a People of great dignity,
Sincerity, and goodness.
Blackrobes were not considered to be outsiders.
Yet they were not Indian.
They hoped to be friends
Who could in some way help the People
To survive.

The Blackrobes, the Chiefs, and the Elders
Had a strong respect for one another.
Prophets from among the tribes
Had foretold the Blackrobes' coming.

But the pride of the men was broken.
Their hearts were sad, confused.

243

They felt their powers for leading,
For healing and holding their people together,
To be wounded and waning.

The Blackrobes also had powers;
They taught a new spiritual Way.
The grandparents agreed with this Way;
It seemed much like their own.

The Blackrobes and Sisters would
Run schools for the children
To teach them the new powers
That could come from knowing
Letters, numbers, books.

All this helped a People move
Into a new age. The Chiefs, the men and women
Prayer Leaders, the Catechists,
The Church Builders and Doormen,
All worked together with the priests,

But the old Circle of Powers was broken.
It was not so shared anymore.
It appeared that priests and Sisters
Had a greater part of the circle
Of spiritual powers for leading and helping.
The People felt more receiving than giving,
Being told rather than listened to.

All this was happening in a world
Where Indian Ways came more and more to be
Criticised, condemned, ignored.
And the Circle has remained broken
Even to this day.

The Sense of the Sacred

There have been many men and women saints,
Many holy Prayer Leaders
And good, selfless Chiefs.

But the feeling grew strong
That holiness was more in the priests,
Brothers and Sisters,
Than in the whole People together.

The sense of the Sacred
Grew more confined to those things
Within a Church or in things carried:
A rosary, a medal, a picture.
The sense of the Holy
Being in all things was lost.

The Circle Restored

Today there is a new feeling of strength
And self-direction among the People.
It would be good if the Circle of Powers
Were made whole again.

It would be good to see again
Men and women, Elders, priests, deacons and Sisters
All equal in sharing in the circle of gifts
For helping the People.

It would be good to sit down together,
To listen to the Elders,
To listen to each other's hearts,
To consider, to choose, to pray
For a way of traveling together
Best for the whole People.

This Would Be a Circle and a People

This would be a Circle of men and women
Who feel they are sons and daughters of their Creator,
Brothers and sisters in Christ,
Full of reverence for the Holy
Present in all Creation.

This would be a People full of trust
In each other and in their Maker,
Together facing and choosing a path
From the past into the future and the totally unknown.

3. The Gifts Among the People Today

"There is a variety of gifts
But always the same Spirit;
There are all sorts of service
To be done, but always to the same
Lord: working in all sorts of
Different ways in different people . . ."
1 Cor. 12:4-7

The Way the People Are

Within the Indian people today
There continues
A great depth and dignity,
A spiritual Presence and powers
That have been theirs for thousands of years.

This simply is the way the People are,
Something the Creator has given them.
The People are Alive!

They know extreme pain
And great joy,
Disharmony and harmony,
Losing and finding.

The People are still in touch
With the main currents of human life,
And because of this they are in contact
With the Source of Life.

Indian Elders speak
From the heart,
From felt and seen knowledge,
From a calm and steady center.

Elder men and women prefer
To speak and act deliberately,
With a clear and studied view
Of the nature and needs of everyone
And everything around them.

The Many Spiritual Gifts

Within our communities today
We have many spiritual gifts.
There are the Elders in each community
Whose lives of silence and prayer
Seek the betterment of everyone.

The Grandparents' lives of Faith
Are clearly real.
Their lives are an example and hope
For their children and grandchildren.

We have holy men and women who can heal
Sickness in mind, spirit, and body.

We have those who build for us,
And support our work together
With dinners, raffles, turkey-shoots,
Bingo, fund drives.

We have our cooks
Who feed us when we come together
To remember dear ones,
To pray for help,
To laugh, to cry.

We have those who visit and comfort the sick,
Those who travel to see those in prison,

Men and women who give up
Weekends for kids' basketball
Or to take 4-H'ers to the County Fair.

We have our political leaders,
Educators, conservationists, economists,
Social workers and nurses,
Game wardens and policemen,
All who work to preserve and build
The People's future.

Sometimes when the Bishop comes to join us,
We try to honor all these ways
Of helping and giving,
By calling leaders forward
And blessing them with thanks
Before all the people.

SPECIAL ROLES WITHIN THE CHURCH

Helping Roles

Within the Church we also have
More formally recognized ways
Of reaching out to help all people.

There are Catechists in each community
Who work with parents and with the young,
Eager to share their Faith,
Hoping to show a good Way to the children.

There are Acolytes,
Men who work with the priest
In bringing the Sacraments to the People.
These men help to give the Mass
Its full dimension and dignity.

They are good men
Asked by the priest and Elders

To help the People.
They can lead a Communion Service
And bring Communion to the sick.
They can baptize
And help lead the graveside prayers.

Often Elders will help the priest and Acolytes
By bringing Communion from the Sunday Mass
To ailing members of their own family at home.

We have Readers
Who read from the Bible at Mass
And help to teach the Faith.

We have Song Leaders, Choir Leaders,
Musicians, all who help the People in prayer.

There are Doormen who welcome the people
To Mass and Communion, men who help
Keep good order and dignity
In our Masses and Funerals;
These men sometimes wear a sash
Over their shoulder.

There are Prayer Leaders
Who lead the songs and prayers for the dead,
And Speakers who express the People's heart
At wakes, Burials, and Masses, as well as
At all sacred and special dinners and gatherings.

There are Sisters
Whose whole life is a sacrifice and prayer of love
To Jesus for His People.

The Sisters are always working,
Instructing the young and adults,
Helping parents to teach their children,
Visiting and caring for the elderly and the sick,
Bringing Communion to shut-ins,
Joining in and helping in any way they can
To build up the life of the towns they live in.

Ordained Roles

There are Priests and Deacons
Ordained by the Church to help
Lead the People at Mass
And share with them all the Sacraments of the Church.

They are meant to participate in all
That brings life, growth, wholeness to a community.
It is their duty to take a stand
Against anything that kills the People's Spirit.

The Priest

It is a priest's life to be a pastor, a shepherd,
One who leads by word and example,
One who seeks out, encourages, and supports
All those working together to bring
Joy and deep peace into the community he serves.

The priest, in a special way, represents the Bishop
Who, in a complete way, represents Christ
Present among and caring for His People.

The Bishop is a special sign
Of the gifts of leadership and authority
Given to the Church by the Holy Spirit.
The Bishop shares these gifts of authority and leadership
With the priests and deacons
Who work with him for the people.

It is the priest's duty and joy to help bring
All the Sacraments of the Church to the People.
Christ and His Body, the Church, both on earth
And in heaven, works through him to
Baptize and confirm,
To lead at the Eucharist,
To forgive sins,
To affirm and bless marriages,

To make the sick well,
To console the dying.
It is his life especially to seek out
The hidden, the forgotten, the hurting.

The priest's whole heart is meant to be for Jesus
And for His People.
The two are inseparable for him.

He should live out the Mass he says daily,
Willing to give his life for the Life of the People.
He should be a man of patience with himself and others,
Knowing the time it takes for a person to grow.
Death and sorrow
Are his constant companions;
He must be able to hear and absorb endless pain
And to humbly release it to Jesus on the Cross.

He must continually learn
From the People he serves
So that they can learn to trust him
And give him their hearts in return.
He should come to know the limits of his strength,
His need to share his work,
His need to rest, to pray, to read.

The Deacon

The Deacon is one whose whole life
Is to help others.
He should be a mature man
Whose love for Christ and concern for his own People
Is clear and shining.

The deacon's special concerns are care for the elderly
And protection for the young.
He should be someone whom the young admire
For his way of life,
And someone they can go to for guidance.

Deacons baptize.
They assist at Mass, reading the Gospel
And sometimes giving the homily or talk.
They lead the People at Communion Services,
Bless marriages
And lead graveside prayers.

Someday soon there will be more priests and deacons
Chosen, from among the People, for their goodness,
Their lives of self-sacrifice,
Their integrity and truthfulness,
Their desire to be an example for the young.

All Are Sinners Yet Called to Help

These are all men and women from the community,
Helped by the community,
To work for the life of the community.

They are all sinners,
Carrying the weight of their sins,
And they are close companions of Jesus.
Their days are filled with prayer and self-sacrifice.

They hope to be with Christ
And with the Creator's holy ones,
Their Grandparents, both in this life
And in the world to come.

4. There is Only One Priest

"Since in Jesus, the Son of God,
We have the supreme high priest
Who has gone through to the highest heaven,
We must never let go of the faith
That we have professed."

Heb. 4:14

There is really only One Priest,
Jesus, who in obedience to his Father
Laid down His life
For the Life of the world.

And we who participate in this Mystery
Through the power of our Baptism in His Spirit
Are all priests, who with Him
Lay down our lives
For the Life of the world.

The Bishop and the priests
Who work with Him for the People
Are in a special way the Presence
Of the Priesthood of Christ among us.

Bishops and priests preside at Mass,
Greatly honored to lead and to bless.
They are an important part
Of the whole Priesthood of Jesus Christ,
A Priesthood we all share in together
As Christ's body on earth.

The priesthood of the Bishops and priests
Enables us to live our priesthood,
For strength and wisdom come to us
From meeting Jesus in the Sacraments
And seeing Him in the witness of their lives.

And when we live our priesthood,
Sharing in the work of Jesus,
We encourage and enable priests and Bishops
To live their priesthood more fully and joyfully.

We all share in Jesus' Mission
To bring the Life and Light of God
More and more into the world,
A world locked in struggle with Evil.

One Priest

There is really only One Priest
In whom the whole universe was made
In a wonderful manner.
Coming forth from our Creator,
He has fully entered into our world
And made His home here.
He wishes to fill our whole world
With the gift of His Spirit.

We hope to participate in this adventure
By dying to anything but the Goodness,
The Fullness of Light that our Maker wishes
To pour into us and, through us,
Into the whole world.

We suffer and die trusting in Him.
We believe the Life He has given us

"Will turn into a spring inside . . .
Welling up to eternal life." Jn. 4:14b

We hope to walk with Him in this life,
And return with Him to the Father,
In a wonderful manner.

5. He Will Never Leave Us

> *"Blessed be God the Father of our*
> *Lord Jesus Christ, who has*
> *Blessed us with all the*
> *Spiritual blessings of*
> *Heaven in Christ. Before*
> *The world was made, he chose us . . .*
> *To live through love in his presence . . ."*
>
> Eph. 1:3-4

Jesus, The One Coming Towards Us

There is, in the end,
Amidst all of our hopes and strivings,
Only one thing that truly matters,
Only one great Reality:

Our Creator coming towards us
In the Presence of Jesus.

Because our Father lifted Him up
After He had emptied Himself for us,
He now lives totally in all things.

He is Love everywhere Present to us,
Coming towards us, the complete
And total gift of Himself.

This is His Eucharistic Presence in our world,
Centered in the Blessed Bread
We share at the Mass.

It is the Reality of Jesus' Presence
In our hearts
And in the very heart of the world
That is the Source of all goodness and light.

Our confidence in Him can be limitless
Because He is limitless.

We will never have to live without Him,
Because, simply, we can't live without Him.

He Is Like No Other

Jesus is like no other.
He goes beyond any particular
Time and history.

This is why Paul
Who never saw Jesus in the flesh
Could become His greatest Apostle.

This is why the early Church,
In the midst of her ongoing, changing situations,
Could dare to interpret and declare
The meaning of Jesus' life on earth.

The early Church continued to experience
The ongoing miracle of Jesus' Presence
And the Presence of His Spirit.

The Church through the ages
Continued to enjoy the gift of His Presence.
And today it is no less possible
For us to meet and come to know Him
As if for the first time.
Jesus!
New, Vibrant, Alive,
Very much aware of us
And wishing to be part of the story
Which we call our history.

He Is the One We Are Going Toward

We are living now because of Him.
He is the Source of all our joy, that joy
Which is the gift of His Spirit to us.

And if the world as we know it
Should pass away tomorrow,
It truly doesn't matter,
Because we firmly believe
We are held forever in His Heart.

We trust Him.

And it truly does not matter
Whether we are great or small,
For our lives now and our destiny
Are the same:
Jesus, our Lord, Today!
                    Tomorrow!
                    Forever!

And the only questions of true importance
Remain the same:
Did we free, release, give away
The goodness, creativity, and light
That He placed burning, bursting inside of us?

Was he born again in us
And given back without reserve to the Father
And to all of our brothers and sisters?

6. It is Good for Us to Gather Together

*"For where two or three meet in my name,
I shall be there with them."*

Mt. 18:20

It is good for us to gather together
To support each other,
Encourage each other, especially when
One of us is down
And doesn't want to continue.

It is good sometimes
For just the men to be together
To talk, to pray, to eat together,
And sometimes Sweat and fast together.

It is good sometimes
For just the women to gather
So they can consider their need
To be a blessing to each other.
This must be if they are to continue
Serving and helping so many.

It is good sometimes
For just the young to be together
To enjoy each other's company
And begin to speak of their dreams,
Daring to be the unique persons they are.

It is good sometimes for just couples
To be together, to share a moment for themselves,
To see each other anew.
The example of others working at a marriage
Gives life to a couple tempted to lose heart.

Sometimes it is very good
To gather everyone, all families,
Grandparents to grandchildren,
Not just for funerals,
But also for memorials, dinners, birthdays,
Anniversaries and Feast Days. On these days
There is the strength of a common Faith,
That this is a great People together
Making a journey home.

It is good for Tribal Leaders
To meet together and pray,
Asking guidance and listening deeply
To each other's heart.
This is so no one is forgotten,
And the People are guided towards Life.

It is good for us to have someone
To pray with, to speak our heart to.
There is great strength in two praying together.
The Spirit, as promised us, does come to help us.

There is immense strength when the whole People
Gather in prayer for healing.
The Spirit is often poured out
Upon the whole gathering,
And no one goes home the same person.

It is good for us to feel free
To pray for each other,
Joining hands as family, as friends,
As husband and wife.

It is good to lay our hands gently
On someone hurting,
And humbly ask Jesus to help them.

We have this hope
That whenever we pray together
In this life,
Those who have gone ahead,
Our Ancestors, pray with us.

7. To a Young Person Dreaming of Becoming a Leader for the People

"I heard the voice of the Lord saying:
'Whom shall I send?
Who will be our messenger?'
I answered, 'Here I am, send me'."

Is. 6:8

"If anyone wants to be first,
He must make himself last of all
And servant of all."

Mk. 9:35

What Do You Want to Be?

Do you have the desire in you
To become a leader and serve the People?
What does that mean to you?
Will you give yourself
To petty politics, only
Out for what you can get
For yourself, your family?

Or do you wish to be
Like the great Chiefs
Who led by good example?

A great Chief was someone for the People
To see, to listen to,
To remember forever.

The Great Chiefs

The great Chiefs took nothing
For themselves. They only wished
To give away what they had,
To sacrifice themselves for their People.

They did not look for reward or praise.
They began and ended each day
With prayers of thanks,
And prayers for the health of everyone.

Their hearts went out in concern
For the Elders. They were one in mind
And heart with their Ancestors.
They kept the Way of Life intact.

The great Chiefs were firm,
Yet gentle with the little ones,
Scolding, encouraging, teaching.
They wanted the young to know how
Self-discipline and self-respect go together.
They were someone for the young to see.

Can You Walk This Way?

Is this the Way you wish to follow?
Can you walk a straight path
Between the fires of jealousy, the back-biting,
Anger, frustration, despair,
Hatred, doubt, suspicion,
That will surely surround you?
Have you the heart for this?

Or will you give in to egotism,
Deception, lies, lust,
To the desire for
Drink, sex, money,
When the pressure is on,
When you feel the weight of responsibility,
The lure of comfort, control, prestige?

Do You Have the Strength for This Journey?

Have you the strength in you
To walk a path seeking the Truth?

Or will Evil take away your purpose,
Strip you of your strength,
And break you into pieces?

You do have the strength,
And you don't have the strength.
Your real Strength will come to you
Through your prayers and fasting.

It will come to you through your efforts
To walk in honesty and humility,
And, when you fall,
In your ability to get up
And begin again.
Your real Strength will come to you
Through the prayers of your Ancestors,
Who are one with you.

Your real Strength will come to you
Through your response
To the sacrifices and prayers
Of all those who truly love you,
Your large family, the living Church
That surrounds and upholds you.

*   *   *   *   *   *

There is much more that could be written
About the gifts of the Spirit
To the Church,
Christ Present in His People,
Reaching out to help all Peoples
On their journey Home;
But let us end here for now.

8. An Historical Note on the Gifts Of Leadership Within the Church

> *"Each one of you has received a special*
> *Grace, so, like good stewards responsible*
> *For all these different graces of God,*
> *Put yourself at the service of others."*
>
> 1 Pet.9-10

The Gifts of the Spirit

From the beginning, the men and women who gathered to-gether to follow Jesus' way of living experienced themselves as filled with powers: power to love the earth and each other, power to hope in the Creator and in each other, power to believe in the Father and His Son, Jesus, alive and present in the world and in each other.

They felt set free within themselves new powers to understand, to study, to pray, to see, to hear, to feel, to reach out, to help, to teach, to forgive, to heal, to change. These powers they ex-perienced as given to them.

These men and women who believed in Jesus felt changed; they felt full of life, and energy and hope. They felt as if a new heart had been given them. Blind before, they now could see. Unfeeling before, they now could empathize. Their stopped-up ears now heard. Once trapped within themselves, slaves to their desires, they now were freed to care, to love.

Once victims of darkest despair, they were now filled with a hope they could not even explain. Once helpless in the face of sickness and death, they now acted decisively against the power and control of Evil in the world. All of these real gifts of power they experienced as from the Spirit of the Creator, the Holy Spirit, the Helper promised and sent by Jesus, their Elder Brother, through the power of His death and resurrection.

The Gifts of Prayer and Helping Out in the Early Church

Within the early communities there were as many roles or ways of helping out as there were people. Everyone tried to share what he had and looked out for one another, no one trying to have more than anyone else. Members of each community tried to wish one another well, solve differences, forgive one another, and pray for one another as well as for the other communities.

Believers gathered together to pray, to read the Scriptures, and to break the Blessed Bread together. In this Eucharist and in this whole Way of Life, Jesus became very real to them, as did the gifts of His Holy Spirit. They felt as if He acted through them to help the world grow through its suffering. They felt as if they were now His Body on earth. They felt as if they were a People moving ahead together on a journey through suffering, death, and rejection to a more abundant Life for everyone. Those who had gone ahead, the Saints, prayed for those still walking on. Along with all the gifts of prayer and mutual help given to the early church, there were also gifts of authority and good order given by the same Spirit. Within the Christian communities strong roles of leadership and service began to emerge.

The Gifts of Leadership in the Early Church

There were Bishops, successors of the Apostles, working men, sometimes married men, chosen by their communities to lead in the communities' lives of faith and worship. There were Presbyters or Elders, often men married and with a trade, chosen by the community to advise the Bishop, and also to offer the Eucharist when the Bishop could not be present.

Deacons were selected by the community to take care of the material needs of the people. They were married, working men, perhaps the busiest of all the leaders. Deacons read the epistle and gospel at the Eucharist, received the offerings of the people, and helped the Presbyter give out Communion. The Deaconesses cared for the women of the community, looking out for the sick and poor, teaching the Good News, helping at the Baptisms of women.

The Doorkeeper kept right order in the church. The Cantor, or Song Leader, intoned and led the liturgical music of the people.

Each person received the Eucharist by hand and some helped bring Communion to the sick. There were also teachers and prophets, and some with the gift of healing. There were many couples devoted to family life, wise in directing and building up the strength and life of the whole community.

In the second century, the word *priest* is used for a liturgical leader, rather than the words *presbyter* or *elder*. Acolytes are mentioned in Rome in the third century. Their duties were to take care of the candles, carry the Eucharist in processions, and help at the Mass. Lectors read the epistle and sometimes the gospel at the Liturgy. The role of Exorcist was practiced in the Church by the third century. The duty of the Exorcist was mainly to heal the possessed and the sick.

The Growth of the Priesthood Within the Church

As the Church grew larger, these roles within the believing community were seen differently. The Bishop became more of an authority figure, ruling over a part of the Church.

Roles of leadership within the Church took on the image and manner of leadership in the secular world. Bishops and the Pope became both spiritual and temporal leaders, helping to hold together the very fabric of society. They belonged to an ordered world in which royalty, the ruling class, was seen as separate from the common man. As the Liturgy became a more formalized rite which the faithful watched from a respectful distance, the priesthood took many other roles into itself. By the Middle Ages the positions of Doorkeeper, Lector, Acolyte, Exorcist, and Deacon became steps leading to the priesthood. The priest gradually became a person set apart with special authority and powers as Christ's special representative to the world, rather than a man, fully part of his community, chosen to serve that community together with fellow leaders and helpers.

The Church Today Restores the Many Gifts of Leadership

The Church, especially since the Second Vatican Council, has wished to encourage and restore all roles of service and leadership within the Christian community. That is why today in most Dioceses there are three-year preparation programs for men asked to be deacons. Also, we see priests and Bishops working closely together with:

Acolytes— who help the priest and people at Mass and the other Sacraments, and bring Communion to the Faithful.

Lectors— readers at Mass and at other times of prayer.

Teachers— who bring the Good News to the young and to adults wishing to enter the Church.

Prayer
Leaders—who help the People during Wakes and Funerals, speaking at dinners and whenever the people need them.

Song
Leaders—those who lead the People in song and prayer when the People gather together.

Bringers— who bring Holy Communion to
of the the sick and shut-ins.
Eucharist

Prayer— men and women who, through their
persons life of prayer, bring healing to
and the troubled and the sick in the community.
Healing
persons

The Church Continues to Rediscover Herself

Down through the ages, the Church became very many people. All over the earth, each person, each family, each tribe, each nation tried to express in its way the mystery of their Creator's Life within them, their love of Christ, their way of following Him.

In the Western Church, led by the Pope in Rome, powers for leading and helping out gradually grew to be considered more present in the Bishops, priests and sisters than spread out among the people. The feeling developed that priests and sisters were somehow more holy than the "ordinary" faithful. It was felt that priests and sisters taught, directed and "saved" the "common" people, who were more apt to be sinners. Holiness, authority, teaching, direction were seen as coming down in a vertical line from the Pope through the Bishops, priests and sisters to the people.

Nowadays, there is a strong feeling to return more to the ways of the early Church, when holiness and gifts of leadership, teaching, and helping out were seen as more circular and spread out, belonging to the whole people. Today the Church reaffirms each person, united to Christ through Baptism, as a unique and special gift to their community and to the whole Church. No one wishes to lord it over anyone else, for we are, after all, brothers and sisters, working shoulder to shoulder, each with a special role to help make our world a better home for everyone.

9. Some Prayers

Prayer of St. Francis

Make me a channel of your peace:
Where there is hatred, let me bring your love;
Where there is injury, your pardon, Lord;
And where there's doubt true faith in you.
Make me a channel of your peace:
Where there's despair in life, let me bring hope;
Where there is darkness, ever light;
And where there's sadness ever joy.
O Master, grant that I may never seek
So much to be consoled as to console;
To be understood as to understand;
To be loved as to love with all my soul.
Make me a channel of your peace:
It is in pardoning that we are pardoned;
In giving to all men that we receive;
And in dying that we're born to eternal life.

Take and Receive

Take, Lord, and receive all my liberty,
My memory, my understanding, and my entire will,
All that I have and possess.

You have given it all to me.
To You, Lord, I return it.
Everything is yours; dispose of it
According to your will.
Give me only your love and your grace.
That is enough for me.

A Prayer for Those Who Need Courage

Dear Lord, teach me to be generous;
To give and not to count the cost;
To fight and not to heed the wounds;
To work and ask for no reward,
Save that of knowing I am doing
Your will. Amen.

A Prayer for Those in Stress

God grant me the serenity to accept
The things I cannot change,
Courage to change the things I can,
And wisdom to know the difference.

chapter ten

PRAYING

A Way of Being in the World

1. Naming the Holy

In the Name of the Father, and of the Son,
And of the Holy Spirit. Amen.

We call
The Holy Mystery
The One at the Center
And Origin of all things

Father!

We call
The Life within all things
The Energy moving from within
Breath of all that is born and lives

Spirit! Holy Spirit!

We call
The Presence
The One coming towards us
In Love and Forgiveness

Jesus!

It is He who gives us
All things good, lasting, beautiful.
His Bread is Life for us.

We do not have to worry
Whether they are there
These three
Father, Son, and Spirit.

They simply are,
Like the message hidden in leaves
Suddenly translucent
With a burst of light from above.

It is all true.
It is all given.
They seem to wait to be discovered
Silent, shy, hidden

Yet ready to rush
With the power of a thousand oceans
Into and through a heart
Yearning to feel, to see, to love.

Glory be to the Father, and to the Son,
And to the Holy Spirit. As it was
In the beginning, is now, and ever shall be,
World without end. Amen.

2. He Belongs to This People

"Before anything was created, He existed,
And He holds all things in unity."

Col. 1:17

"It is written in the prophets:
They will all be taught by God,
And to hear the teaching of the Father,
And learn from it,
Is to come to me."

Jn. 6:45

It could well be
That Jesus,
Who was sent into our world
By the Creator, God our Father,
Belongs in a special way
To the Indian People.

From the beginning
Their hearts were open to Him.
From the beginning their hearts
Were straining to meet Him,

Their eyes searching for Him at dawn
On the far horizon.

Jesus is uniquely their own,
And they welcomed Him and His power
To love and forgive.

He was always with them,
Yet He came into their world
Through His body, the Church—
His Church, always good,
Always human and sinful.
The Grandparents kept their hearts focused
On the Head of this body, Jesus.

Jesus is uniquely their own
Because they have suffered greatly.
They have been humiliated, emptied out.
They have been poor, tortured, and despised.
Yet they have endured.

He is uniquely theirs
Because He embodies their desire
To stand beautiful and strong,
Pure without sin before the Maker.

He is theirs
Because He gave His life
For everyone, for every living thing,
Respecting His Father's will for Him.

He is their own
Because He obeyed His Elders
And was raised in a good manner.

He is theirs
Because He was born and cleansed
By water and the Spirit.

He knew how to pray and fast
Alone in the high places.
His hands, His whole body
Were for healing.

He belongs to the Indian Peoples
Because he loved family and children.
He was whole and good
And had time for everyone who came to see Him.

He belongs to them
Because He was an impeccable warrior
Of the Spirit, who fought egotism
And selfishness, accepted great pain,
And laid down His life for His friends.

He is theirs
Because He lived simply
And shared everything he had,
Sharing His own Life
Through the Bread broken
And given around.
He is one with them
Because He was gentle and kind
And welcomed the total stranger
Into His family.

He is their own
Because He spoke truth from the heart.
He loved the hills and streams,
The sky and trees and all the animals
That lived there.

He is theirs
For He could pray all night
And greet the dawn
In humility, confidence, and power.

Jesus belongs to the Indian People
Because he dreamed of living forever
With His holy Ancestors
In a world complete,

Yet not too much different
From our own. He dreamed of a new world
Where there would be no more
Sadness, sickness, or death.

He is uniquely theirs
Because the Grandparents saw clearly
That His Way was their Way,

That His Truth was their Truth,
His Life was their Life,
No matter how much some members of the Church
Or any other people misunderstood this.

3. He Is With Us All the Time

"In the beginning
The Great Spirit was everywhere,
Also the bad spirit.
The Great Spirit was the Divine Providence;
The evil spirit was evil and destructive.
This was until the native lands were changed
And Wahee spoke no more.
Some named him Wanconda
Or the Great manitou.
From the giant water's edge
Strange ones came,
Bad medicine, too."

Clara Covington

"Yahweh, you examine me and know me,
You know if I am standing or sitting,
You know my thoughts from far away . . ."

Psalm 139:122

Prayer can be looking for someone,
Someone you miss, someone you need.

You go up alone into the hills,
Walking among the rocks and trees,
Everything is speaking to you.
You feel Someone is with you.

You walk the forests of the streets
Alone at night.
You stumble from place to place,
Hungry, troubled, empty,
Your stomach, your heart yearning
For someone, something.

The only answer: silence,
And the soft light of the tavern,
The muffled shouts and laughter.

Inside there is the stink
Of beer and sweat,
But at least someone is there
To stand next to,
Someone, maybe, to go with
Who will help you forget the kids at home.

"Am I not Christ's subject?
Why then do I crawl about
Like a curious serpent?
Why must I search for stale waters?
In the beginning
How did the illiterate Indian
Get his tavern and all the boorishness
In that new, wet, smelly, spiritual bundle
Of booze. How did this come?
In Christ's name?
Which Indian leader
Made it to be this way?" Clara Covington

In all of this searching
There is the possibility of finding,
For He is with us all the time,
He, lonely, hurting, looking for us.

He is with us when we're
Wedged between our buddies
In the back seat of a car.
He is in our swollen lips
And with us when we cry alone
At night in the dark church,
"Are You there?"

And sometimes, when we're feeling better
We begin to See
That His concerns are really ours!

"Lord, what can I do to change?"
"What can I do to help my People?"

4. Our Need for Forgiveness And Healing

"In the world you will have trouble,
But be brave: I have conquered the world."
John 16:33

In Our Heaviness

Our sins, our failures, our falling short
Of what we hoped to be and do,
Tell our feelings
That our relationship with our Creator has changed.

We feel estranged, separated, unclean,
Unworthy to be in His Presence.
It is as if we had lost His friendship,
That we are turned away from Him,
And He is turned away from us.

We no longer call Him
Creator, Father, Grandfather.
We no longer dare to call Him
Dad, our Dad.

We feel that everything has gone dead.
The closeness, even the lines
Of communication have been cut.
We are here alone;
He is somewhere else.
His Light no longer shines on us.

This experience of loss
Is not totally bad or useless.
We share this experience
With all men and women in the world.

This feeling of loss
Is very important, for in this situation
We learn to leave ourselves
And begin to lean
On our Creator's boundless love and mercy.

It is in this situation
That we experience an important aspect
Of our Creator's being Creator, and of us being us.
We learn that we are far from perfect
And need much time to grow.

He Comes to Meet Us

It is often in our most dark
And heavy moments
That Jesus comes to help us,
Reaching out to console us,
Embracing us as His blood brothers or sisters.

This is so wonderful,
So inconceivable, so unlike
What our mind, our feelings,
Tell us about ourself.

We dare not look up.
We dare not enter the room
And stand before Him.

Nevertheless, He comes to help us.
He is there, fully faithful,
Fully Himself.

We Dare Not Look Up

We dare not look at Him
To see how He looks at us.
But if we do look, we dare to draw
Out of ourselves.

We are drawn beyond the limits
Our feelings impose on us,
The conditions our mind has set for us,
The judgments we or others have made
About the value of our existence.

If we do dare to look at Him
With steady eyes full of trust,
We are drawn, as if for the first time,
Irrevocably into
The world of Life,
The region of Light,
The place where His Heart lives.

He Speaks to Us

Jesus can speak this word of forgiveness,
This word of welcome,
Directly into the center of our being,
Anywhere, any time.

He can speak it
On the streets or at home,
Between clean sheets or between
The street lights and the gutter.
It doesn't matter.

All that does matter
Is the Word spoken,
The Hand given,
The Heart opened,
And a man, a woman, a child
Can begin to live again.

This Presence of Jesus
Warms and heals us
From the inside out,
Recreating us with His Spirit
Who is poured through us.

We are made totally new,
From nerve fibers to feeling,
Body, mind, and soul.
Our limited life is changed
Into His unlimited Life.

This Presence of Jesus,
This Word of Love and forgiveness extended,
Comes to us directly
Or through the love of others.

For many of us
This experience of love and forgiveness
Comes through the Sacrament of Reconciliation.
Jesus, working through His Body the Church,
Beholds us broken and in tears.
He listens to us, consoles us,
Forgives us, assures us we are worth something.
And we are reborn!
We begin again.

For many of us it is after
Intense prayer with our People
That the Spirit makes His Presence known to us.
We ask to be forgiven, to be healed.

The People pray for us,
Place hands on us
With great kindness and care,
And we are changed!

The Spirit of Jesus
Flows over and in and through us.
We are reborn, strengthened, renewed!

He Asks Us to Sit Down and Eat

There is also the Dinner
That Jesus invites us to.
He Himself is the Food
Given to us for our strength.

We come to this Dinner
To offer our lives as little
And as broken into pieces as they are.
We keep our eyes on the Host
Who has invited us.

At this Meal
We can be forgiven,
Nourished, refreshed,
Through the prayers of our brothers and sisters.

And the great Love Present helps us
To forget our unworthiness,
And rescues us from the delusion
That we cannot begin again.

5. Limits

Our Struggle

It seems as if our whole lives

Are a struggle against limits.
We hate to give up our hold
On what is here and now present to us;
We hate to leave what we know,
Our family, friends, all the gifts
Of the good land and the good People
We are familiar with.

But we must; we cannot hold onto
What we are and have.
Our relationships with all persons and things
Are continually changing.

We struggle with the limits of our mind,
Our heart, our body, our spirit.
We do what we can to be creative,
Free, healthy, strong,
To be all things for our family,
For our People.
But we continually fall short of our goals
And, as we gain years,
Some powers of our mind and body weaken.

Our Peace

Yet the Love placed by the Creator
In our hearts expands,
And inside we are filled more and more
With gratitude for each passing moment.
We become happier with the joy and mystery
Of all created things,
And more hurt by the cruelty of humankind
Towards one another and towards the earth.

In this way our Creator loves us
And prepares us for our Passover
From death to eternal Life,
Either the small daily deaths to selfishness,
Or the final Death when we close our eyes
In this body for the last time.

This is the meaning of Jesus' Passover,
A passage through death to Life Forever.
We find hope in His Passage,
That no matter how painful our deaths,
We will pass over from death to Life with Him.

We grow to trust
That after our death
Our heart, mind, body, spirit,
Will become one with the Heart,
Mind, Body, Spirit of Jesus.

We dare to hope
That we will become as Unlimited as He,
Free to be Present to everyone and everything
We have ever loved,
No longer limited by time and place.

This hope, placed deep in our hearts,
Is our Creator's free gift to us.
This is why we feel that
When those die who are dearest to us,
They become Free and Unlimited,
Present to us everywhere,
All the time.
We believe that where Jesus is
There they are with Him,
And Jesus is Present to us everywhere, all the time.

This is why we feel Peace
Even in our sadness,
And, to our surprise,
The Presence of kind and consoling Love
Even in the midst of our anguish.

"Courage! It is I!
Do not be afraid." Mt. 14:28

6. A Way of Being in the World

"Your Father knows what you need
before you ask him."
Mt. 6:9

A Lesson We Forget

It seems to be a lesson we learn
Again and again:
Prayer is more being someone
Than doing something.

Prayer is more the way we are
Than what we have to offer.
If we are not kind to ourselves
And others, if we are not sensitive
To everything that is,

If we do not care enough
About the people near us
And all the people of the world
To make sacrifices for them,
It will be hard for us to pray.
There are no gimmicks to prayer.

It is most important for us
Just to be ourselves.
That is just fine.
We don't have to be someone else
Or do something else.

Some Things We Can Do

It is important for us to be
Quiet
Attentive
Clear
Simple

Trusting and dependent
As a child before grandmother or grandfather.

It is important for us to become
As a child who loves
Without any conditions at all,
Who needs only to be loved.

It is important for us to leave behind
What weighs us down and buries us,
To leave at the door our guilt
And unworthiness, our worries about our value
And the future of those dear to us.

It is important for us to just for a moment
Let everything go, relax, and simply
Be in the Presence of the Holy Mystery.

The Gifts Within Us

There are the two great gifts in each of us;
A great hunger and searching to find Him, and
A strong feeling and knowing with our whole self
Of a Wonderful, Holy Presence.

We find this Holy Presence in the present moment.
We remember meeting this One
In many ways before.
We look forward to knowing this Person
More in the future.
But the most powerful place we meet Him
Is NOW!

It is important to love and trust Him enough
To give Him time to show us
Our heart as it really is,
Open, transparent to Him as to no other.

It makes no difference
Whether we are sitting or standing,
Walking or lying down.
All that matters
Is that we feel our yearning for Him
Or enjoy the sweet power of His Presence.

Ways of Being With Him

We can talk to Him silently,
Our thoughts communing with His.
We can talk to Him out loud,
Telling Him how we feel,
Full or empty,
That we miss Him.

We may laugh tears of joy and thanks;
We may cry tears of sadness.
Some days, walking, we may sing to Him
Or simply groan
Because we cannot express the pain
Of our union with Him
And our Hunger for Him which happen
Both at the same time.

We may be given the grace to see
All things as gifts
With Him at the Center,
All things coming forth from Him,
He within ourselves,
And in all things large and small.
We can reach out and touch Him
In the unique and wonderful texture
Of each person and thing.

We can listen to Him
In the wind, the streams,
In music and in the quiet trees,
The sea of sound
We are always immersed in.

We can taste Him
In the goodness of food
And feel Him in the tenderness
Of a baby's cheeck.

We can smell Him
In the fir and pine forests,
In the moist earth after summer rain,
In camp coffee, and in the evening hills
Of rolling sage.

We can breathe Him
In the sharp mountain air.
All things are in Him;
He is in all things.
If we look for Him
And want to know Him,
He will not disappoint us.

It is His desire to reveal
His whole Self to us,
Suddenly or gradually,
He, Himself, Jesus,
Hidden, wonderful
In all creation.

Sometimes it is good to be alone,
Sometimes it is good to be with others,
To stand up for Him,
To lift up a hand or join hands,
Enjoying a feeling, a thought,
A word, a song together
In the Presence of our Lord.

It is important sometimes to think hard,
To try to think something through.
There is power in this.

It is also important to let the mind go,
To give up thinking, to rest,
Remaining thankful for everything,
Especially what we cannot understand or control.

Letting Go

It is important for us to feel
Delighted
Loving
Sad
Empty
Worried
And also to let these feelings go.

If we cling to achievements, successes,
Failures, friends, family,
Sickness, health, pleasure,
Pain, life, death,
We hold them back from being
What they truly are,
Simply all a part of our journey.

Nothing else is our Creator except our Creator.
All life, like a river continually moving,
Flows forth from Him,
Is held in being by Him,
And returns to Him.

It is important for us to have
And to share what we have.
It is good to enjoy what is good and beautiful
And it is good to give it away.

We came forth from our Maker with nothing
And we will return with nothing,
Except what we are.

When We Are With Him

Sometimes, when we are with Him,
Our mind races over
A thousand thoughts, images,
A thousand feelings.

We are tempted to dwell on those that
Frighten us or give us pleasure.

It is good for us, then, to return
To our original emptiness,
Like a bowl emptying itself
To receive something.

Most of the time when we are quiet,
It seems nothing important is happening.
We are just there.
He is there.
Yet that is a miracle
If we could only see it!

Though we are usually unaware of it
He is there at the very Center
Of our being, nourishing us,
Building our inward Self, our Spirit.

Yet while this incredible Work is being done,
We seem so unimportant to ourselves.
We try to think how to present ourselves
As someone important, a clown
Before a King.
Sometimes we will be overwhelmed;
Tears will flood our eyes, our hearts,
Tears of sadness for our sins,
Tears of amazement with the fact
Of His Presence, His Love.

Other times we will seem alone.
We will feel afraid to go on,
Abandoned, dying,
Only our Faith holding, sustaining us.
We cry out, "Lord, help me!
I am dying!"

Slowing Down

It is difficult to slow down;
We are always moving so fast.
It is strange,

But we must slow down
So that we can become alert enough
To realize how much is happening
In and around us.
It is like slowing our car enough
To enjoy the beauty of our journey.

But there is a basic fear in us
Of slowing down, becoming quiet.
We fear that if we do slow down,
There might not be Anything
Or Anyone there.
Just NOTHING
Except our fear.

And we are terrified of meeting our own self,
For we fear this self will not be good,
Lovable and capable of love.

These two fears:
The fear of our ultimate ugliness,
And the fear of the Dark Abyss,
The Enemy of our nature uses against us
To keep us from slowing down
And becoming quiet.

Yet if we are helped and encouraged
To slow down, to let go,
Even for a moment becoming quiet,
We may discover sweet Silence, Goodness,
And the indescribable Peace of knowing
That there is nothing for us to be or do
That will ever earn Love.

There is simply Love!
We swim in it,
Are held in it,
Given Life from it,
Like a fish swimming in the Sea.

Holding and Being Held

This is why it is so important for us
To be held, to be respected, supported
From the time we enter the world
And all the way along.

A hug, an embrace, a regard,
A look, a word that gives life,
All of these are needed,
So that a person can Believe.

This is why it is so sad
When someone has never been held and loved,
Bonded to this good earth.
It is then so difficult for that person to believe.

Some Things It Is Good to Do

It is always good to give the day
To our Creator in the morning.
To stand before the sun
After washing in cool water,
Welcoming the Light into us,
Asking for help and forgiveness,
Praying for the health of all those dear to us.

During the day it is always good
To thank Him for food, family, and friends,
To find Him in our work
And in all of the people we meet.

In the evening, before sleeping,
It is good to let our mind calm down,
Taking time for a walk, a smoke, some tea,
To give thanks for the day.

If there is worry, anger, frustration,
It is best to speak to Jesus about it,
Asking Him to free us from these things
Or to help us see them new
In the morning light soon coming.

Sometimes it is good for us
To read the Scriptures.
Some days the words will seem dead to us,
Usually because we feel tired or dead.
Some days the words will dance with Life for us,
The fire of our spirit fanned into Life
By the Fire of His Spirit.

This reading is like eating rich food.
It is best to take a little bit slowly.
If we do not eat this food
Our spirit grows weak and dies.

It is good to say slowly
The prayers of our childhood,
Considering each word carefully
With our whole mind.

It is good to hold a Sacred Word in our heart
Like *Father, Jesus, Grandfather, Spirit.*
We can say this Word in our heart
When we have become quiet.
We can carry this Word like a powerful song
Within us wherever we go.

Because Our Creator is Present
In everyone and everything,
There is no one
And no thing that is unimportant.

Everyone and every thing carries
A power within.
Everything is important.

The War Within and Around Us

There is much weakness, much selfishness in us.
There is much Evil at work in the world.
It staggers us;
We hold our hand to our mouth in horror.

But we must not let our terror,
Our fear of annihilation immobilize us.
We must not be overwhelmed by Evil
Or give in to it. We must not let
Evil stifle our imagination for the good,
For a better world.

Our Quest

Because Jesus trusted,
Because He sacrificed,
Because He didn't give up,
We dare to love, to plan,
To go ahead with confidence.

We cannot give up fighting.
This is our struggle, our quest.
We are not alone. He has suffered
And He is with us. He has given us
His own Spirit to take our side and help us.
He knows there is more against us
Than just our own weaknesses.

And someday, perhaps, when we are old
And covered with wounds,
Our hearts worn out with hoping,
Someone new and young will come to us saying,
"Grandmother, Grandfather,
Teach us how to pray!"